We use intuition to make some of our most important decisions and judgments in life, and yet in spite of this we know little about intuition.

The Intuition Test is designed to force you apply your intuition to make decisions and judgements. The book provides over thirty problems for which there is no logical right or wrong answer. The aim of each problem is to get you to experience your intuition directly. The more familiar you become with the intuitive mind, the more you will hear it when it speaks, and the more confident you will become about using it.

If you want to develop your understanding of intuition, this is the book for you.

The Intuition Test

From gut-feeling to insight

By Jim Blackmann

Nascent State Publishing
Bath, England

First published November 2016

ISBN: 9798663896597

By the same author:

Nascent State Magazine

www.jimblackmann.com

Nascent State Publishing
Bath, England

The Intuition Test

Introduction

*You are walking along a dark road in an unfamiliar
neighbourhood. There are terraced houses on either
side. As you pass one of the houses, you notice the
door is open and a light is on. You notice a broken
plant pot inside the door. You walk up to the door
and you see the doorframe is broken. You look inside
and see the furniture is overturned and damaged.
There is a kitchen knife on the floor and some blood
on the knife. You are just about to phone the police
when you hear a muffled voice coming from a back
room. It sounds like someone is in pain. You call out
but they do not answer back. Would you go in?*

We use the word 'intuition' to describe many things;
we use it to describe gut-feeling, our first impressions
of people, why an action seems right to us, and to
explain our fundamental beliefs in life. All of these are
commonly associated with the term 'intuition', and to
a certain extent all of them express what we mean
when we use the word, but none of them actually tells
us what intuition is.

The purpose of this book is to outline the nature of intuition; its purpose, uses and applications. The aim is to provide the reader with a clear understanding of intuition, how it works and what it does.

We use intuition to make some of our most important decisions and judgements in life, such as choosing a career, finding a partner, or moving to a new home. We use it to deal with people, pick up on moods, and to cope with unexpected situations and events where the outcome is as yet unknown or uncertain. We resort to intuition rather than to logic to make such decisions and judgements because logic deals with right and wrong, and many of the more important decisions in life provide us with no clear right or wrong choices. So, when we are confronted with an important event, a difficult situation, or a decision which will affect an unknown future, we use intuitive judgement to decide what to do.

In spite of this we know very little about intuition. We are born with a degree of intuitive ability and we assume it will be there to serve us when we need it. We have a much better understanding of logic. This is because we are trained to think logically at school; indeed, logic informs the whole of the present-day education system, and through that, all the legal, economic, political and scientific institutions of the present era. Logic is so dominant Western culture that many people regard it as the only legitimate form of thinking. Because of this many people dismiss intuition as inferior to logic, and as little more than an expression of a confused emotional life. But intuition is much more than just bad logic or confused emotions, and is as much a part of our thinking as reason or mathematics.

The word 'intuition has the same root as 'tuition'; just as a tutor watches over us as we study, the intuitive mind watches over us as we think and feel and act. When we have second thoughts about an action we are about to take, or when we suspect that we are missing something very important, or when we feel we have to take stock of our life, it is the intuitive mind watching over us, prompting us to consider what we are missing, and drawing our attention to what we cannot see directly.

Because we use intuition for so many of our major decisions and judgements in life, it makes sense to try to understand it, to know what it is and to know how and when to apply it. By developing our understanding of intuition, we will improve our ability to use it.

The approach taken by this book is one of direct experience rather than of theoretical explanation. That is why the book is called *The Intuition Test*; the purpose of the book is to test your intuitive ability. The book provides you with thirty problems for which there is no obvious right or wrong answer. Each problem will test your intuitive ability by preventing you from applying logic to arrive at a solution. This is not the same as a school exam, where you receive an overall score, but rather like a test to challenge your ability to apply intuition to make a decision or judgement. The more your intuitive ability is tested, the more familiar you will become with its nature.

The book will begin by outlining the nature of intuition, by providing a broad description of the way the intuitive mind works, and then go on to cover the different aspects of intuition, from gut-feeling through to observation and then insight. The chapters that follow will then provide more details about each of these elements, before going on to say something about intuition and its application to the different aspects of life.

Owing to the dominance of logic in society, there is a chapter on logic itself. Logic effects the way we see the world whether we are aware of it or not, and so a good understanding of logic will provide the basis for seeing both its benefits and its faults. Logic is useful for so many things - from law to economics and to politics - but it is not useful for other things, such as dealing with complex relationships, the emotional life, or with decisions where the outcome is uncertain. We need to know when to apply logic and when to apply intuition, and to do so we have to have a good understanding of both.

There is also a chapter on the unconscious mind. There is much about human nature which is not wholly rational; we are not always aware of the causes of our actions and, in some cases, our motives for taking them, which are often unclear and unconscious. Although we prefer to regard ourselves as rational, it is better to understand this side of human nature rather than to deny it. Intuition is the means to understand the unconscious mind.

While logic deals with what we know and see, intuition deals with what we do not know or cannot see directly. There is much that we do not know – the future, other people's motives, and the hidden laws of nature – and yet we live with the unknown and yet rarely pay attention to it. To this end there will be chapters on deception, illusion and enigmas. We use intuition whenever we come across anything in life which is puzzling, perplexing or confusing.

Because we use intuition on a daily basis – forming judgements about people and making decisions which will affect the course of our life – there are chapters on the application of intuition to decision making, judgements and people-watching.

As well as the outer world – people, events and life-decisions – there are also chapters on how we relate intuitively to the inner life, such as to the emotions and to matters of conscience. Conscience and the emotions play an important part in life, and they operate very differently from logic.

Then there is a chapter on the important subject of insight. An insightful idea can often arrive as though from nowhere, and suddenly change all that we thought and knew about a situation. Insight has played an important role in science, invention, and indeed in our wider understanding of the world, and yet it is little understood. This is because insight is intuitive and it works very differently from conventional logic.

And finally, there is a chapter on the outcomes, methods and practice of intuition. If we want to understand intuition, and we want our understanding of it to be more than just theoretical, then we have to be able to apply it in everyday life. Just as logic has its own methods and outcomes, so too does intuition. The application of intuition will be outlined at the end of the book when the different aspects of intuition have been worked through in some detail.

If we ignore our intuition, we will still use it anyway, but we will use it badly. We may confuse it with prejudice or with subjective emotions, or with the feeling of being right. Most of our bad decisions are based on seeing too little, on not being in touch with our emotions, or on not considering the motives for our actions clearly enough. And the problem with bad decisions is that we have to live with them.

Once we recognise the importance played by intuition in everyday life, it makes sense to try and understand its nature. Where something as essential as intuition is concerned, theoretical understanding is not enough; it is important to practice and develop it in a viable way, much in the same way we might practice and develop a musical skill or an aptitude for mathematics. We are taught to think logically at school, and many of its principles and practices are second nature to us, but intuitive thinking is not taught at all. In order to balance this one-sided approach to education, we will need to focus from time-to-time on developing our intuitive ability.

The aim of this book is to provide the reader with a practical understanding of intuition through direct examples of its use, its methods and its applications. If you want better intuition, this book can help.

The Intuitive Mind

You are a soldier in a war. There is a sniper firing at you and you are trapped behind a low wall. There is a volley of shots, followed by a silence. Then there is a second volley of shots followed by another silence. You come to the conclusion that the sniper is stopping to reload, and so you wait for the next volley of shots to end before taking your chance. Another volley follows, then you reach up over the wall and fire a series of shots back in the direction of the sniper. This time the silence is longer. Finally, the sniper cries out in pain. They call out again and again with increasing agony and then curse you, plead to God for mercy and then it goes completely silent. Would you look up over the wall?

We have to make many decisions in life, some simple and some complex. The simple decisions are usually choices between right and wrong; should we report a misdemeanour to an authority? But there are times when the right course of action is not so obvious or clear-cut; if the misdemeanour was committed by a close friend, would we still report it? Complex decisions mean we have to consider the outcome, and if the outcome is unknown, then we have to think twice before making it. The problem with such decisions is that it is often only after the event that we can know whether the choice we made was the right one or not, and by then it is often too late to change it.

We are taught to think logically at school, from a very early age. Logic trains us to think in terms of right and wrong. In a multiple-choice exam, for example, we are presented with a question and four possible answers. We work through each of the answers and try to find fault with them; the answer which has no obviously faults becomes the right answer. This is logic. The problem is that while this works well in school exams, it doesn't work so well in life.

We can employ logic for many of the lesser decisions in life, particularly those which involve dealing with something we are already familiar with. We know how much we can spend and stay within our budget. We know what time we have to start out from home to be on time for work. We can use logic for lesser decisions of this kind because we are dealing with familiar situations where the outcome is known. So, when we are dealing with routine decisions, 'right' becomes what worked in the past and 'wrong' becomes what didn't work. Routine decisions of this kind make up a large part of life, and logic is fine for them. But when the routine is interrupted in some way, such as when an emergency requires us to spend beyond our means, or when the decision involves changing a routine, such as finding a new job, then right and wrong become more difficult to define, and logic fails us.

This is why we use intuition rather than logic to make some of our more important decisions in life. Our more important decisions involve making choices which will bring about a significant change in our day to day routine; should we move to a new town, start a new career, or end a relationship? When we are dealing with an unknown outcome, we often have to make the decision with too little information to be certain if the decision is the right one or not.

When logic fails us, we have to use intuition. We rely on gut-feeling to make some of our most important decisions and judgments in life, from dealing with people to deciding our future to looking at our own motives for taking an action. Intuition is at least as important as logic, and in some respects more so, and yet for all of this we have little understanding of what intuition is or what it does.

The word 'intuition' has the same root as the word 'tuition' and it means 'to watch'. The intuitive mind watches over us just as a tutor watches over us as we study. So, the intuitive mind is the watching mind.

We do not just think and speak and act, we observe ourselves as we do so. It is because we can observe and monitor ourselves, both inwardly and outwardly, that we can change our behaviour. We can reflect on what we have done in the past, watch as we act in the present and then think about how we might behave in future. If we could not monitor and observe ourselves in this way, we would be condemned to repeat the same behaviour over and over again. It is true that we can use logic for some of this; if bad behaviour got us into trouble, or if we overspent in the past, then logic can tell us this was wrong. But there are many occasions when right and wrong is not so clear-cut - when we are about to say something inappropriate, or when an enjoyment has become an indulgence, or when a discussion has become a heated argument – and the judgment is based on context and balance; then we employ intuition. Intuitive judgment is the activity of the watching mind.

We use intuition not just to observe the inner life, but to observe and monitor the outer world as well. We can observe people, events and nature intuitively. For example, we might listen to a person speaking, and wonder about the motives behind what they are saying. We might watch the build-up to war, and focus on the emotions that fuel the conflict. Or we might observe a wildflower, and wonder how nature can produce such a wonderful blend of colours. The intuitive mind picks up on the hidden and less obvious elements of life. It could be said that the watching mind sees what the eyes cannot see.

The logical mind, on the other hand, can only attend to what we see and know directly. This is because we can label and define what we see and know, but we cannot label and define what is hidden from direct observation. We can label a person as a friend because we have observed their past behaviour towards us. This will not however tell us how they well behave in future. We note a landmark because it is familiar to us; another landmark will go unnoticed because it has yet no label. Logic deals with the world we know and see, and it deals with it effectively, but we cannot label what we do not know or cannot see.

Your friends have recently had a baby. They invite you along for a celebratory meal with a small group of friends at their home. You go along; the company is bright and the conversation is engaging, and many topics are discussed during the course of the evening. Then the parents bring up the subject of the birth. They say that in some cultures it is traditional to cook and eat the placenta. Indeed, they say, this is regarded as a form of celebration, and an important part of the birthing process. Then they go into the kitchen and return with the cooked placenta on a platter, garnished with onions, mushrooms, herbs and gravy. Would you eat it?

There are many things in life we do not know or cannot see directly. We cannot see the future, the inner life of others, the laws of nature and even many of our own deeper and hidden motives. We often act for reasons which are not clear to us at the time, and only though hindsight does this become apparent. So, when we are dealing with an unknown, we resort to intuition. If logic deals with the known world, intuition deals with the unknown in life.

In addition to the unknown, we also use intuition to deal with the many elements of life, both inwardly and outwardly, which are not subject to logic. Such elements tend to be complex, conditional and temporary. We pick up on a humorous remark and respond to it in kind. We may not speak of politics in mixed company. We may find ourselves walking through a park on a sunny day and stop to take in the enjoyment. Such decisions are intuitive.

If the world was logical and people were rational, logic would be enough to deal with life; but of course, people are not wholly logical and life is not always subject to reason. As for ourselves, our actions are often coloured by emotions, desires and aspirations, not all of which bear logical scrutiny.

Many of the major decisions in life involve thinking about outcomes which are unknown at the time of the decision. The problem with the unknown is that it affects us emotionally, which is why fear, hope and anxiety all arise whenever we are faced with a decision involving an unknown, whether it is meeting a stranger, starting a new job, or ending a relationship. The unknown is like a darkened room. We do not like walking into a darkened room; we prefer a world which is visible and known.

We find it difficult to rely on our intuition because we have never been taught to think intuitively. The education system focuses on logic, mathematics and grammar, and it ignores intuition. We assume that it is enough to be born with a natural intuitive ability and that this innate ability will serve us well when we need it. We assume that in times of stress or uncertainty it will magically kick in and help us make the decision. This is like expecting to be able to play a piano without training, or to add and subtract without being taught how to do so. So, if we want to be able to use our intuition effectively, we have to be willing to learn how to use it and practice it directly, just as we would with any other ability.

In order to improve our intuition, we can begin by understanding its nature; what it is and what it does, and we can do this by studying it directly. The direct study of intuition is the approach taken by this book. The purpose of this approach is to force the reader to apply intuitive judgement, and in this way to experience the intuitive mind directly. The more familiar we are with the way the intuitive mind works, the better we will be able to understand it and the more confident we will be about applying it when the time comes.

This approach has many advantages. The first advantage is that the reader doesn't have to take anything on trust; any statement made about intuition can be checked against the reader's own experience before it is accepted or rejected. The second advantage is that by continually practicing intuition, we will become increasingly more familiar with its voice and nature. Theoretical explanations are fine for logic, but not for life. Life requires intuition if we are to understand it at all.

Intuition is part of the inner life, and for this reason, we cannot study it in the same way we might study a flower or a rock. Studying our own inner nature can be more difficult than studying the outer world; the outer world has an objectivity that allows us to return to the flower or the rock the next day and find it much the same. Intuition is ephemeral. Carl Jung, who co-founded psychoanalysis with Sigmund Freud, wrote in his *Psychological Types* (1921):

'Because, in the main, intuition is an unconscious process, the conscious apprehension of its nature is a very difficult matter.'

For this reason, a slower and more deliberate approach to the study of intuition is necessary. Each of the problems presented in this book will give the reader a first-hand opportunity to experience their intuition in action. Repeated experience will allow the reader to develop a greater familiarity with the intuitive mind and its nature.

Intuitive thoughts can appear vague and imprecise. This is in part because we have been trained to think logically, and we expect our intuitive thoughts to be as clearly stated as logical thoughts. If someone makes a logical error – that a penguin is a fish - we can point to the fault in the thinking. In the same way, if we want to demonstrate our knowledge of a subject, we will find the correct terms and references to make our point. Logic is fixed and precise; we know that an apple is not a vegetable. But we cannot deal with our intuitive thoughts in the same way, because intuition speaks with a very different voice; an intuitive thought is more like a sudden insight than a rehearsed argument.

The ability to think logically means we have to reduce an experience down to its basic element and then name the element. So, an apple, which includes its taste, texture, colour, size and nutrition, is reduced down to the single term 'apple'. While this is fine for simple items, more complex matters such as social events, relationships and human nature are not well-served by a single label. An enemy soldier may also be a father, a reluctant conscript or a farmer by trade. Intuition will often pick up on the hidden elements that logic misses. That is why intuitive thoughts often cause us to question what we see and know.

There are many things we cannot see directly; we cannot see another person's motives or the causes behind events, or the future. That is why, if someone is trying to deceive or manipulate us, we pick up on it intuitively. It is why, if we doubt an official version of an event, it is because an intuitive thought has prompted us to do so. And it is why we deal with decisions which will affect our future through gut-feeling. If an intuitive thought appears vague or imprecise, it is because it is picking up on that which is vague and imprecise in our experience of life.

This is perhaps one of the key distinctions between logic and intuition. Logic deals with the known world, whereas intuition deals with the unknown or the hidden in life.

In what follows is a brief outline of intuition and its applications in life. There are three elements to intuition; gut-feeling, intuitive observation, and insight. Each of these elements will be covered in more detail in later chapters.

The element most commonly associated with intuition is known as 'gut-feeling'. Gut-feeling is usually described as a sort of anxiety felt in the pit of the stomach at a time when we are about to make an important decision. Although gut-feeling may tell us that we feel uncomfortable about the decision or judgement, it will not always tell us why. This can be a problem, because we know that our gut-feeling is telling us something, but we cannot examine what it is saying exactly, and it is for that reason gut-feeling is regarded as vague and imprecise. None the less, gut-feeling will tell us there is something we have not yet seen directly.

We apply intuition for dealing with the emotional life. Logic wants us to see the world in black and white, but the emotional life is fluid and changing and varied. We can go from being mildly irritated one minute, to outright angry the next, to being ashamed of the outburst a moment later. Whereas an opinion can survive over many years and even over a lifetime, an emotional reaction has a much shorter lifespan.

Logic cannot deal with the emotions because the emotions do not conform to the rules of logic. From the point of view of logic, a contradiction is wrong and must be eliminated. The emotions however contain many contradictory qualities. We can sit outside an interview room and feel both hopeful and fearful at the same time. We can be angry at someone and still care about them. While emotions are subjective, they are nonetheless real, and affect our actions as much as the ticking of a clock or the need for water. If we find it difficult to pin our emotions down to a single definition, it is because the emotions do not conform to logical analysis. It is for this reason that we say the head is telling us one thing and heart is telling us another.

The emotions are not the same as intuition, but they are associated with intuition because intuition is best suited to dealing with them. To be more in touch with our emotions, we have to be more intuitive. Being intuitive doesn't make us more emotional, it just makes us more aware of the emotions that are there. That is why our more important decisions are intuitive, because what we feel about a decision is as important as whether it is logically correct or technically right.

We also associate intuition with the imagination and with fantasy. Emotional terms such as 'love' or 'terror' are often accompanied by an image, whether it is a fantasy or a nightmare. Our imagination plays a much more important part in life than is generally imagined; we dream in the day just as we do at night, but we do not see our daydreams because they are overlaid by our more powerful daytime experiences. While dreams and fantasies may not be real, they can often influence what kind of career we will pursue, what kind of person we are attracted to, and what kind of world we want to live in. Again, our imagination is not rational or logical, and so it is the intuitive mind that picks up on this aspect of our inner life.

Intuition is also employed in our judgements in life, towards people and events. Intuitive judgement operates very differently from logical judgement; it is slower, and because it is slower, it allows more time for new thoughts and new insights to arrive. That is why if we resist the temptation to make instant or snap judgement, we may find ourselves in receipt of second thoughts, which can often appear out of nowhere. We may be engaged in a mundane activity, such as washing or cleaning, and then suddenly find that we have an insightful thought into the nature of what had been bothering us. Such thoughts will often shed light on what our gut-feeling had alerted us to, but couldn't tell us what it was. We may have been troubled by another person's motives, or by a decision we were about to make, or by some uncertainty about our own motives for an action. If we pick up on the initial gut-feeling, and do not rush to judgement, we may find an insight arrives, quite unexpectedly, and provides us with an answer we had half-guessed but couldn't see directly. Insight is intuitive.

Intuition is the watching mind; it 'sees' rather than 'thinks'. If our inner life is complex, emotional and fluid, then the intuitive mind will pick up on this. If we find ourselves in a complex situation with many people and elements involved, the intuitive mind picks up on the complexity, and allow us to deal with the situation as a whole rather than by attaching a singular label and reacting accordingly. Logic is about being right; intuition is about seeing. Intuitive thinking is about seeing more than is obvious in any given situation. This illustrates the key difference between logic and intuition. Being right prevents us from trying to see more, because once we are 'right' we stop questioning, searching, or waiting for new thoughts to arrive.

If we are not clear about what intuition is or how the intuitive mind works, it is because formal education pays very little attention to it. The neglect of intuition is the reason why we don't always hear it speak, or pick up on it when our gut-feeling warns us there is something we are not taking fully into account. Sometimes it is only later, particularly after we have made a bad decision, that we realise the intuitive mind was always there, quietly prompting us, but we weren't listening.

To think intuitively, we have to prevent the logical mind from dominating our thinking. This does not mean taking a negative attitude towards logic, but simply knowing that logic has its limitations.

Perhaps the greatest limitation of logic is that it cannot deal with the unknown, simply because we cannot label what we do not know or see. If we think we see the world in its entirety, that we understand people already, that we are fully in touch with our emotions, or that we can see the influence of dreams and fantasies on our actions, then we can safely ignore the intuitive mind. This book is for those who are not so convinced by logic and who want a better understanding of themselves, others and the world around.

The Logical Mind

You are in a lifeboat with one other survivor from a shipwreck. The sun is setting and it is about to go dark. There are two pairs of oars. You take one pair and start rowing, and then you ask the other survivor to take the other pair. But the other survivor refuses; instead they lie back and try to get some sleep. You remind them that there is no food or water and that you are many miles from shore. You tell them unless they take a pair of oars and start rowing, you will both die of hunger or thirst. But the other survivor says that if you both row together, you will both grow tired together and probably fall asleep together, and if that happens, you will lose your bearings; so, it is better to take turns sleeping and rowing. Who is right?

It might seem odd to begin a book about intuition with a chapter on logic. And yet logic is so dominant, both in our thinking and in society, that it is not possible to say anything about intuition without addressing the influence of logic first. Logic is not just a form of thinking; it is also a way of looking at the world. The application of logic carries with it so many assumptions which influence the way we see the world that it does so even if we do not regard ourselves as particularly logical.

Logic forces us to think in terms of 'is' or 'is not'. It is for this reason that we speak of the logical mind and the intuitive mind as two quite separate and distinct minds. In addition to this, the dominance of logic means that intuition is regarded as illogical and therefore inferior to logic. In order to outline intuition on its own terms, it will be necessary to adopt a somewhat negative attitude towards logic. This might give the reader the impression that to be able to think intuitively we have to reject logic; but this is not so. It is quite possible to think both logically and intuitively, and to be good at both. Indeed, to be able to think well means knowing when to apply logic and when to apply intuition. So, the critical attitude towards logic which runs through the book is for the purpose of countering the dominance of logic, not rejecting it altogether.

Logic has many advantages, otherwise we wouldn't value it so highly or use it so widely. Logic allows us to organise our thinking into categories, rather like the cataloguing system in a library. The problem with this approach is that the simple rule of 'is' or 'is not' forces us to think in terms of opposites. Logic has given us science versus religion, nature versus nurture, ecology versus industrialism, capitalism versus communism, and the individual versus the state. This polarised form of thinking comes directly from the application of logic, and it is applied universally in physics and chemistry, biology and botany, politics and economics, computing and mechanics, and indeed in any area where precision of thought is important.

Those who see the disadvantages and limitations of logic least clearly are the academics who teach it; those who succeed in education do so because they are best able to thinking logically. That is why this book has been aimed at the general reader rather than the academic.

Our experiences of life are often complex and varied, and so in order to apply logic, we have to focus on one particular element of an experience and then attach a label to that element. For this reason, logic forces us to reduce our experiences down to what can be included under a single label. This means that anything which is not included under the label is ignored or dismissed or rejected. This is the reason why a dolphin is a mammal and a shark is a fish, even though they both swim in the same water.

The outcome of thinking logically is that we are forced to see the world in terms of labels; we take the experience of 'pepper', for example, and convert it into the word 'pepper'. And yet our experience of pepper is much more complex than the word itself, and it includes the taste, the colour, the scent, the use of pepper and its effect in cooking. By applying a single label to this complex experience, we can then speak of 'pepper' quite apart from whether we are referring to the scent, the taste or the appearance, or whether it is white, black or green, corn or grain, fresh or dried.

If we could not reduce complex experiences down to a single label, we would not be able to apply the fundamental principle of 'is' or 'is not'. So, the advantages of logic are also its disadvantages. Logic allows us to say that pepper is not salt, or that green pepper is not black pepper, and this allows us to think precisely, but at the cost of a very limited way of dealing with experience.

In addition to simplifying our experiences, logic has a second application; that of organising our experiences into groups. If we define a dolphin as a marine mammal, we can then link it to other marine mammals such as whales and seals. We can then think in terms of 'marine mammals' without having to explain why certain types of sea creature are not included in this group. This form of generalisation has many advantages. Generalising allows us to say that spanners, saws and screwdrivers are tools, and carrots, cucumbers and cabbages are vegetables. It means we can go into a hardware store and expect to find a saw and not a cucumber.

Generalisations of this type are referred to as 'concepts'. Concepts allow us to think of a stool, a chair or a stump of wood as a 'seat', and a knife, a gun or a rock as a 'weapon'. The ability to generalise our experiences into concepts leads to the kind of classification systems found in libraries, law and biology. The naming system provided by Carl Linnaeus (1707 - 1778) in his system of taxonomy, is an example of this form of classification.

As with the principle of exclusion or inclusion, the ability to generalise also has its disadvantages. If we categorise all mushrooms into 'edible' and 'poisonous', then we will begin to see all mushrooms in these terms. It means that if we think of a rock as a weapon, we will not see it as a doorstop. And if we think of a human being as an enemy, we will not see them as a friend.

So, while the ability to generalise is highly useful for classifying our experiences into groups, it can severely limit what we see and how we see it. This can be a problem when what we experience is complex and multifaceted. Human beings and human society are complex systems, where both rational and irrational thinking play an important part in shaping behaviour. That is why, when we deal with individuals and society in terms of labels, we get prejudice and not understanding.

A building has a ground floor, a first floor and an elevator between them. The elevator has the capacity to carry no more than eight people. The elevator arrives on the ground floor with two people on it. One person gets off and two people get on. The elevator then goes back and forth between the two floors and each time it stops, one person gets off and two people get on. What floor will the elevator be on when someone is refused entry?

For some problems, such as the one above, there is clearly only one right answer. This is the kind of problem we are presented with in a school exam. In order to answer the question, we have to take in all the available information and then work through what is presented until we arrive at the inevitable conclusion. The purpose of the question is to test our logical or mathematical ability, and those who succeed at this type of exam often go on to become academics, who then go on to train others to think logically.

Once we leave the academic system however, we soon discover that life itself is not logical. If the number of people who got on and off an elevator always remained constant, then it would be possible to predict when the elevator would not be able to accept any more people; this rarely happens. So, the education system trains us to think logically, but in order to apply the same logic to life we have to assume that logic governs life, but of course it doesn't.

Because the education system focuses on logic, we leave school with a set of assumptions which inform the way we see the world. For example, we assume that if we can find fault with another point of view, then that point of view is wrong and our point of view is right. While the ability to find fault with others is useful for spotting errors in an argument, it is less useful for dealing with people in terms of their emotions, outlook and perspective. In an argument, both people may be partly right because they are both looking at part of the situation, and both may be partly wrong for the same reason. Indeed, reducing an experience down to a single label means this is more likely than not.

Fault-finding of this sort informs all forms of debate and discussion in society, and this can be seen most clearly in the arena of politics. The method of finding fault with another point of view is known as the 'Socratic Method', after the Greek philosopher Socrates (470 – 399 BC), who employed the method to attack anything he regarded as untrue. The same method was adopted by the Church to attack the heresies, which they regarded as untrue. The Church then set up the universities, in Bologna, Paris, and then Oxford, in the eleventh and twelfth centuries. It was through this that logic became the dominant form of thinking in Western culture. Even in the modern era, logic is employed by many orthodox thinkers to attack anything which they deem to be untrue.

The application of the Socratic Method forces us to see the world in terms of right and wrong. If we regard our own outlook or opinion as right, then any outlook or opinion which contradicts our own must be wrong. This not only results in a very black and white view of the world, but it also limits how we see the world. If we are forced to criticise an idea rather than to consider it for its merits then we will be able to see only its faults, even if it does have merits. This is why political parties must find fault with each other, even if the wider population regards the differences as minimal or deliberately exaggerated.

The ability to think in terms of opposites works well in fixed environments, where very little changes. This is why logic works so well in physics. Logic allows us to classify iron, copper or lead as minerals because minerals do not turn into vegetables before our very eyes. The same form of thinking is employed in medicine, chemistry, physics, engineering, economics, law, politics, religion, science, education and philosophy. Where logic is less useful is in our understanding of human nature. This is because human nature is not so fixed; a person can go from being irritated, to angry, to violent and all within the space of a few minutes. It is for this reason that the social sciences, which deal with human nature, are regarded as 'soft' sciences, because human nature does not conform to the rigour of logic.

Human nature is complex, changing and emotional. People can act out of mixed feelings, contradictory views and complex motives. When we apply logic to human nature, it forces us to see a very complex being in terms of a single label. So, if a person is caught telling a lie, then they are labelled a 'liar', even though the lie might have been small and told only once by an honest person. Because logic forces us to divide our experiences into 'is' or 'is not', it means that if we criticise religion, we must be an atheist; if we criticise capitalism, we must be a communist, and if we criticise science then we must be a creationist. Of course, it is possible to criticise religion and still be religious, as did Martin Luther (1483 – 1546), who founded the Protestant movement, and it is possible to be both religious and a scientist, as was Michael Faraday (1791 – 1867), one of the early pioneers in the generation of electricity.

Logic also fails when it comes to dealing with human interactions. If people did not change throughout the course of life, then we could apply a single label and define them accordingly; but of course, people change. What we want as children, and then as teenagers, and then as mature adults, is not the same as what we want in older life. In addition to age, people are guided by emotions, desires and unstated motives which can change according to circumstance. A person can also have regrets about their actions, and this can lead to a change in future behaviour. When we apply logic to human nature, we get fixed thinking, which can lead prejudice, intolerance and conflict.

The dominance of logic means that we accept many of its inherent values automatically and without question. It is for this reason that the failings of logic have to be pointed out, because without seeing them clearly, we might assume the values of logic are correct and then attempt to apply the same values to intuitive thinking.

The relationship between logic and intuition is that the logical mind 'thinks' and the intuitive mind 'sees'. That is why our immediate experience of the world is intuitive. It is only after this that we apply logic and then try to sort our experience into definitions, labels and categories. It is also why, when the intuitive mind is active, we can vary our judgements, but when it is passive, we see the world in the black and white categories of logic alone. It is not that intuition is right and logic is wrong, but that we need both. At present, logic is dominant and intuition is ignored. The aim of this book is to address that imbalance.

The Unconscious Mind

You go to a science convention. There is a foyer lined with stalls and displays showcasing some of the new technologies being developed. One of the stalls is by a leading biotech firm, which is offering samples of some of the artificial foods they have been working on. The first sample is of minced beef made entirely of protein. You try some and you agree that it tastes exactly like minced beef. The next sample is strips of chicken made entirely of vegetable matter. You try some and again you agree that it has the same taste and texture of chicken. Then you are offered a sample of orange juice made entirely of sheep's blood. Would you try some?

We like to think that we make our decisions and judgements on the basis of sound reason and logic. We do not like to admit that many of our decisions and judgements are based on gut-feeling and emotion. To admit such things would be to undermine our belief that we are rational beings. Our unwillingness to admit this however does not free us from the influence of the unconscious mind; our unconscious motives remain as they are, hidden and buried behind the thoughts of our rational mind. Indeed, being unwilling to recognise the unconscious mind actually gives it greater influence over our actions by making its influence more difficult to see.

The term 'unconscious' is used to refer to many different aspects of the inner life; some of them can be verified by a little self-observation and some require a degree of deduction. There are different assertions about what the unconscious mind is, and some are theoretical, but what is not in doubt is that there are elements of the inner life which we do not see clearly. These elements include such things as the emotions, dreams and fantasies, instinctive responses and desires, ambitions, impulses, attitudes and outlooks. A person can be greatly influenced in life by their outlook, and yet be unable to see this clearly. If our outlook is that there should be order in the world, we can become intolerant of others who do not see the world in the same way. If, on the other hand, we take the view that individuals should choose their own course of action, we can become resentful of those who appeal to uniformity and order. We refer to the hidden element of the inner life as 'unconscious', because it includes much that is obscure, indefinite and difficult to define.

Perhaps what makes the unconscious most difficult to see is that it is not logical. Logic allows us to think with precision by attaching a word or term to what we observe, but the unconscious mind isn't clear-cut or defined – our emotional life, for example, is often mixed and confused - and so it doesn't respond well to logical treatment.

Gut-feeling and instinct are often spoken about in the same sense – the term 'gut-instinct' is used interchangeably with 'gut-feeling - but there is a considerable difference between them. Our instinctive responses are constant. We have the same instinctive response to rotten food quite apart from what we think or feel about it. We may feel uncomfortable with a stranger standing too close to us, quite apart from whether we like them or not. Our instincts are regarded as unconscious because we cannot inspect them directly or even alter them by what we think. We may instinctively dislike the rain, even though we tell ourselves it is only rain.

Gut-feeling is associated with instinct because, like instinct, it can dictate how we respond to something without our being able to say why. We may like or dislike a person immediately on meeting them. We may feel uncomfortable in a public place, even though there is no obvious threat or immediate danger. We may walk into a prospective home and immediately like it without being able to say why. Gut-feeling informs our thinking in the same way that instinct informs our thinking, but whereas instinct has to do with pleasure or pain, gut-feeling is more emotional. We may find someone sexually attractive and yet have a gut-feeling about not pursuing a relationship with them.

We can observe our more obvious emotions, such as outright anger or bursts of laughter, but many low-lying emotions such as irritation or boredom will often escape our attention. What makes such emotions difficult to observe is that we cannot apply the 'is' or 'is not' judgement of logic to them. If we undertake a new venture for example, such as starting a business or going on a first date, we will do so with a degree of hope and fear. We can feel angry with a friend and still care about them. Such emotions are not logical; if we try to apply logic to them, we won't get understanding and clarity, but simply a limited view of what is going on inside.

In addition to the emotions, the unconscious mind also includes our dreams and fantasies. Our dreams are highly emotional, which is why the feeling of fear or anxiety can give rise to nightmares. We can reflect on such dreams when we wake up, and realise they are not real, but we cannot wake up from our day dreams and daytime fantasies in the same way. Just as we dream at night, we also continue to dream in the day, but we don't see our daydreams in the same way we do not see the stars in the day; and yet just like the stars, they still exist.

We do just not choose a career or a home or a partner on the basis of necessity, but often with the image in mind of what our life will be like after we have made the decision. Such dreams and fantasies are much more powerful than we realise, and it is largely because we cannot examine them directly that we do not see this. It is interesting to note that the advertising industry appeals almost exclusively to the unconscious mind. That is why celebrity endorsement is employed, because we unconsciously associate the product with the celebrity and the image of success and appeal which they project.

But perhaps the element of our inner life that most evades direct inspection are our moral, or perhaps less-than moral impulses. Just as we prefer to regard ourselves as rational and logical people, we also prefer to regard ourselves as moral and upstanding people. We do not like to look too closely at the darker side of our character because too often it is highly irrational. We do not like to admit that we can be motivated by revenge, jealousy or bitterness because to do so would be to admit that we are not wholly good, and that would prevent us from being labelled as a 'good' person.

Logic does little to help us to see or understand the unconscious mind, mostly because the unconscious is irrational, emotional and complex. In order to see the influence of the unconscious mind over our decisions and judgements, we have to observe our inner life intuitively.

You are a man at a New Year's Eve fancy dress party. You are dressed as a ballerina, and you are wearing tights, lipstick, a wig and a tutu. A fire alarm goes off next door. The fire department arrives and you go outside to see what is happening. The fire officer tells you there might be a gas explosion, and you all have to evacuate the area. They advise you to go down to the end of the road where there is a pub.

You walk down to the pub at the end of the road and you stand outside; there are a dozen motorbikes parked out front, the windows are blacked-out and you can hear loud rock music playing inside. It is cold and you are a man wearing tights, lipstick, a wig and a tutu. Would you go in?

We prefer the world we know; although we are happy enough to experiment and explore, we only do this provided we have a home to return to. It is the same when we are in a situation where the outcome is unknown or when we fear the outcome may not be to our liking. Just as we do not like walking into a darkened room, we do not like to be guided by forces we cannot see. We prefer the feeling of being in control. This is why we prefer routine, familiar faces and known outcomes.

We ignore the unconscious mind because it is something we cannot see clearly. Instead we focus on the routine and the familiar of a day job and a home, with bills to pay and obligations to meet; the unconscious mind, if it exists, can wait for another day. It is only when our routine is disturbed in some way, perhaps with the threat of eviction or unemployment, or a social or political crisis, that the unconscious mind – always there – comes to the fore in our thinking. Just as fear or anxiety can give rise to nightmares, the same can give rise to imagination and panic in daily life. It is when we are dealing with the unknown or the unfamiliar, whether it is the threat of bankruptcy, homelessness, or a troublesome stranger, that we become aware of the unconscious mind and its influence.

Whereas logic demands that we reduce our experience down to what can be known for certain and labelled with accuracy, the unconscious is not clear and defined; it speaks in picture images, in imaginations and in fiery and dark emotions. It is for this reason that intuition is more suited to dealing with the unconscious mind than logic. But to see it as it is, requires our willingness to accept that the unconscious mind is real, and that it influences our judgements and actions. Once we accept the unconscious mind for what it is, we can stop trying to put it into a logical and coherent structure and begin to deal with it effectively. For those who are trained to think logically, this will seem like a kind of defeatism, of giving in to complexity and confusion rather than being willing to make sense of it. But if we want to understand the unconscious mind, we have to be able to focus on moods, contexts and images rather than on specifics and labels.

We pick up on a complex environment unconsciously, through gut-feeling. When the mood in a room changes, or when the seasons change, or when the economic or political climate changes, we experience this initially through gut-feeling. It is for this reason that gut-feeling is sometimes referred to as a kind of 'sixth sense', to distinguish it from the way our ordinary senses pick up on the environment. Rather than attribute any magical quality to gut-feeling, it is better to study it as it is, and to observe how we use it to relate to complex situations and changing environments.

A context is made up of many different elements. A context can be a room full of people, a combination of wind and rain, a political climate, a media storm, or a fancy-dress party. We make our decisions and judgements within a particular context; whether we regard something as good or bad depends largely on the context in which it is made. If we look at a basket of apples, we will choose the best one, even though the same apple might be overlooked in a different basket of apples. We may move into a house near a railway tracks and find the noise unbearable, until after a while we stop hearing it at all. If everyone is wearing a suit and tie and we are not, we will feel odd, and if everyone is casually dressed and we are in a suit and tie, we will also feel odd. All our decisions and judgements are made within a context, but we do not see the context in the same way we see the specifics in the environment.

A context can include both elements from the outer world and elements from the inner life. In the example of the man in the tutu, there is the external environment of the loud music, the motorbikes and their associated culture, the pub atmosphere, the time of year, and the probability that many people inside the pub will be drunk. Then inwardly, there is the fear of association that comes from a man being dressed as a woman, as well as the confidence or lack of it of the individual concerned. All of this feeds into the overall context, and all of it is picked up by gut-feeling.

Because contexts are complex, they can change and develop over time. A dinner party can go from being enjoyable, to a disaster, and yet still include the same elements that made it an enjoyable dinner party. There are formal contexts such as weddings and funerals and divorces. Formal contexts have a degree of stability and permanence, and for that reason we can define and label them as 'weddings', 'funerals' and 'divorces', and then treat them accordingly. But there are also informal contexts, such as a chance meeting in the street, an argument at a traffic light or a quiet bench on a sunny day. Some contexts can be enduring, like a culture or a religion, some can be semi-enduring, like a fashion or a political movement, and some can be short-lived, like the excitement of a group of schoolchildren, or the feeling of exhilaration after a first kiss. Short-lived and informal contexts are more difficult to define than long-term and permanent contexts.

In order to define a context, we have to take one element of the context and then apply a label to it. We might say a gold bar is valuable and forget it is only valuable within a particular context; if we are dying of thirst in a desert, a gold bar is less valuable than a jug of water.

We pick up on contexts intuitively, through gut-feeling. That is why gut-feeling will tell us that a discussion has turned into an argument, or that poor morale at work has become a problem. It will tell us when a statement is inappropriate, or when we need to apply a bit of civility. It will alert us to a change in the seasons, or to the stress we might feel on a busy street. This way of picking up on the context is unconscious, which is why it comes to us through gut-feeling.

For the same reason, gut-feeling will also tell us when a purely logical judgement is wrong. If we are about to make a life-changing decision, such as whether to move home, take up a new job, or to marry or divorce, gut-feeling will pick up on the elements that logic leaves out. This element is contextual, and can include our motives, expectations, emotions, dreams and fantasies. Gut-feeling draws our attention to the very elements that logic cannot see.

There is always an unconscious element to any important decision we make. We have to live with the consequences of our actions, and that means we experience the consequences of any decision personally and directly. Becoming more intuitive means we can take this unconscious element into account before making the decision. It does not mean we will make the right decision, but it does mean we will have a better understanding of why we have made it.

The better our intuition, the better we will be able to see this unconscious element, both internally and externally. Rather than making snap decisions and judgements and then applying a specific and fixed label, intuition will allow us to consider the complexity of the situation for what it is. If a situation is complex, contradictory or confusing, it is better to admit this rather than to deny it. Logic is useful if we want to be right, but intuition is useful if we want to understand.

The Hidden in Life

A woman sits down next to a man on a busy train. The journey is a long one, so they begin to talk. They find out they are both heading to the same city, and they are both about to start new jobs there. They talk about the work they have done, the places they lived and the life they have led. Then they talk about the new city, about what drew them to it, and about what they are expecting from it. They talk about the difficulty of making such a move, of finding new friends and of starting up again. The woman asks the man what his partner does. Why does she want to know this?

The more important decisions and judgements in life involve dealing with an unknown. Whether it is an unknown person, a new situation, an uncertain outcome or information we do not yet have, our more important decisions and judgements involve thinking about either what we cannot see or do not know.

Logic works well when we are dealing with the world we know; if you have had olives before, you will know whether you like olives or not. If you have voted for a political party before then you know what to expect if you vote for the same political party again. We can apply logic to what we know because we can say whether something is, or is not, to our liking. But we cannot apply logic to what we do not know.

There are many things in life we don't know. We can, for the most part, ignore the unknown because life provides us with plenty to keep us busy. We have day-jobs, social commitments, bills to pay and homes to keep, and provided none of this is interrupted, we can deal with the world by attending to what is familiar and known. And yet, even if our routine is not interrupted, the unknown plays a much more important part in life than is generally imagined. We do not know whether we will remain healthy, whether we will be burgled, whether our day-job will last, or even what our friends really think of us; all of this is commonplace, and it affects us unconsciously, which is why we take out insurance, save for a rainy day, lock our doors at night, and speak politely to our friends and acquaintances.

We do not even know ourselves as we should; many of our deeper motives are hidden from us and we only see them clearly, in hindsight, long after the time when we were prompted to act.

When we do have to consider the unknown, for example when we have to make a life changing decision, we first try to apply logic; this is because we have been trained to think logically, and we feel more confident about using this method than using intuition. Logic tells us to weigh up the pros and cons, to dismiss anything we regard as irrelevant, and then try to decide what is the most important factor in making our judgement. The problem with this method is that it ignores any unconscious elements, both internally and externally, which will affect our judgement.

The logical method is not unlike a gambler in a betting shop; a gambler will study the past form of the horse, the ability of the jockey, and the strengths and weaknesses of the competition, then check the weather conditions and the racing course, and then finally put all this information together to make an educated guess about the outcome. Studying the form in this way should improve the gambler's chances of winning, but it does not mean they will actually win, simply because the outcome of a race is often determined by factors not available to the gambler, such as whether the jockey is having marital problems or whether the horse has a mild case of colic.

The logical approach to dealing with the unknown informs many of our judgements and decisions in life. We will ask for a CV from a prospective employee because we believe this will tell us whether they are reliable and honest, or study a brochure and then research the locale before buying a new home. With the logical approach, we try to gain as much information as possible so that we can project what we know on to what we do not know in the hope this will give us an accurate picture of the unknown.

Much of our thinking about the unknown takes the form of assumptions. For the most part our assumptions about the world serve us well. We assume that if we do not break the law we will not go to prison; we assume that if we live within our means we will not go into debt, and we assume that if we pursue a healthy lifestyle today, we will remain healthy tomorrow. Provided our assumptions are not tested, we can live with any number of them and not regard them as such.

The logical method works for the most part because life is stable. If what worked in the past works today then we expect that it should work tomorrow. But there are times when life doesn't work out as we expect, when a crisis or an unforeseen interruption to our daily routine forces us to think again, or our assumptions prove to be wrong, and then we have to rely on a different method – more often than not, gut-feeling – to make our judgment. When this happens, we have to consider the unknown directly. Indeed, it is only when the unknown does not conform to our expectations that we actually see it for what it is.

You live in a block of flats. There have been two burglaries inside the block in recent weeks. The main door has an intercom system and it limits access to strangers, so you begin to wonder if one of the other residents is responsible. You think about the different residents in the block and you begin to form your suspicions about one of them. Then early one morning you go downstairs and you see some morning mail lying just inside the door. You go through the envelopes to see if there is one for you, and you notice there is a letter for the resident you suspect as the burglar. The envelope is marked 'Important Summons' and it is badly sealed. Would you look inside?

As much as we might tell ourselves we act logically, many of our actions are motivated by emotion, instinct and desire. What we call a 'problem' involves dealing with the unknown, and what we call an 'answer' means finding the missing information which will allow us to stop thinking about it. If the missing information is in a book or a vault, then it is simply a matter of gaining access to it in order to solve the problem. Most academic, medical and scientific research is based on this method; conduct a detailed study and hope information alone will solve the problem. But if we cannot gain access to the information we need – if the vault is locked or the book is unavailable - then no amount of research will discover it, and we have to employ a different method.

This can happen when the information is deliberately hidden, such as when a code is employed to transmit a message, or when secrecy is employed, either by individuals, groups or organisations. Hidden information plays a key role in life. A person who has made a serious error may deny it. A company negotiating a contract will not openly state their bottom line. A man who is attracted to a woman may tell her he is just being friendly. Secrecy is used for both honest and dishonest means, and it is very much a part of life.

There are also occasions when we cannot gain the information we need because the information does not exist. This can happen when we are dealing with a new situation; we can only know whether a new venture will succeed or not after we have tried it. And there are occasions when information is there but no one is looking for it; for example, electricity generators, vaccines and telescopes could have been invented long before they were, but what prevented them was the assumption that our existing knowledge of the world was sufficient.

If the information exists but it is not known to us, then we can use logic. But if the information does not exist or if it is actively hidden from us, then then we have to use intuition. Just as there is a logical approach to solving problems, there is also an intuitive approach to solving problems.

Our initial response to an unknown situation or to hidden information is through gut-feeling. Gut-feeling will tell us there is something we cannot see directly, but it will not tell us what it is. Once we become aware of the gut-feeling, we begin to search for the hidden information. If a person is trying to deceive us, or if we are about to act recklessly, or if we are provided with a limited explanation for an event, our first suspicions come through gut-feeling. We might feel there is something not quite right about what is being presented, and gut-feeling will draw our attention to the hidden element.

Gut-feeling is the dim realisation that there is more to what we see than meets the eye.

Because logic wants us to think in terms of right or wrong, it simplifies experience by focusing on the most obvious features and labelling them. While this provides a form of closure, it prevents us from considering the less obvious features present in the situation. It follows that if we want to focus on the hidden element, we have to prevent the logical mind from dominating our thinking. This is why the intuitive method is slower than logic; it considers not just what is obvious, but also what is unobvious. At the very least this means keeping an open mind, or better, it means being willing to actively consider unorthodox ideas for what they might reveal about the hidden element. This way, the intuitive mind will provide us with new thoughts and insights quite beyond the limited perspective we have at present.

The problem with hidden information is that it does not jump out and announce itself to us. We have to actively seek it. If we are willing to be open-minded, and if we are able to hold off an immediate logical judgement, and if we are patient with the intuitive mind, we may find ourselves in receipt of new thoughts and insights.

Intuitive ideas are more like inspirations than coherent arguments. The reason for this is that the intuitive mind expresses itself in terms of images rather than in terms of words. That is why inspired ideas such as inventions, novels and songs are more like picture images rather than reasoned arguments. An inspired thought will emerge as if from nowhere, and often in a whisper, not unlike Echo of the Greek myth, when she whispered to Narcissus.

Intuitive thoughts can occur at any time. They do not arise out of logic, but more often when the logical method has failed us or when we have grown tired of it. It is when we give up trying to collate what we know and focus on something else entirely, such as when we have a break from thinking about the problem, that intuitive thoughts tend to arise. It is owing to the nature of intuitive ideas that they appear unexpectedly. We have to attend to the whisper, which appears as little more than a possibility, and then nurture it before it becomes clear and obvious.

We live with hidden information. The future is hidden, the laws of nature are hidden, the forces behind social events are hidden, and the inner life of other people is hidden. Many of our own darker thoughts and motives are also very unclear to us. The phenomenon of hindsight can reveal this to us; we may see after the event what we could not see at the time of the decision. The hidden is part of life, whether we are aware of it or not.

If we want to be right, then logic is fine. If we are happy with our understanding of the world, of others and ourselves, then logic is fine. But if we have the gut-feeling that there is more to the world than meets the eye, that people are not always what they seem, and that life presents us with many enigmas and unknowns, then we have to be able to think intuitively. If we do not consider the hidden, then we can mistake a very limited view of life for the truth.

Deception

You work in a warehouse at night. The shift-manager smokes. The warehouse has a no smoking policy, but there is a changing room at the back where the smoke alarm doesn't work. You go into the changing room at the end of your shift and you see the manager's cigarettes and lighter. You decide he won't notice if one is missing, and so you take one and light it up. Then you hear the shift manager in the hallway outside, and so you put the cigarette out in a bin. The next day you turn up for work and you discover the warehouse has been severely damaged by fire. The police are at the scene; the shift-manager's lighter has been found in the changing room where the fire started, and he has been charged with arson. Would you say anything?

It is not necessary to tell a lie in order to deceive. In order to deceive, it is merely necessary to leave out information. We can examine the information provided, but we cannot examine the information which is not provided, or missing or hidden. So, the art of deception is to present limited information and make it look whole and complete. To do this it is necessary to ensure that the hidden information is never suspected. We will only look for hidden information if we have a reason to suspect it exists.

Logic deals well with existing information. We can examine what we know and then scrutinise it to see whether there are any errors. But logic cannot deal with missing information because we cannot scrutinise what we do not know or cannot see.

We pick up on deception intuitively. Our first suspicions that a deception is taking place begins with gut-feeling. We observe what is happening and, unless the deception is clumsy, we may have little more than the gut-feeling that something is not quite right. We may be unable to say exactly what it is, but none the less we can know the gut-feeling is there. When this happens, it can provide us with the incentive to look beyond what is presented and try to discover what is presently hidden from us.

We recognise that there is a difference between what a person says and why they are saying it. A person can pay a compliment because they admire someone or because they want a flatter someone. A person can report a crime because it is their duty or because they want revenge. A person can call their friend an 'idiot' because they want to criticise them or amuse them. Logic can examine what a person says, but logic cannot examine their motives for saying it. That is because motives are hidden, and in order to see motives we have to think intuitively.

A lie is the most obvious and common form of deception. Many lies are told to avoid punishment or embarrassment or to gain an unfair advantage. For this reason, many lies are told on the spur of the moment, and are often no more than clumsy attempts to pass off an untruth for truth. It takes little or no talent to lie, and so a clumsy lie can be examined for inconsistencies, inaccuracies or omissions, and this can be done by applying logic.

But there are more developed forms of deception, and the discovery of such methods requires more than simply spotting an obvious error or untruth.

A more developed form of deception is like a forged banknote. A forged banknote will have all the appearance of a real banknote, and it will pass off as the real thing until it is examined closely. For this reason, a good forger will seek to prevent the banknote from being scrutinised in the first place. The speed of the transaction, a distracting smile, or its inclusion with a bundle of real banknotes will all help to prevent the forgery from being scrutinised until after the transaction has taken place. What is most important is that the deception is not suspected, because this would trigger unwanted scrutiny. So, with a more developed form of deception, what matters is not just that the lie has the appearance of truth, but that the lie is not even suspected at all.

The most effective means to prevent a lie from being scrutinised is to control the attention of the person being deceived. The art of controlling attention is practiced to a high degree by stage magicians, through a practice known as 'misdirection'. The stage magician knows the audience will want to see how the trick works, and so they will use this curiosity to their advantage. They will invite the audience to 'watch closely' as the trick is performed; but the more the audience looks in the direction indicated, the less they will see where the real trick occurs. This is because the trick is never in the direction indicated by the magician, but elsewhere. The problem is not in the ability of the audience to pay attention, but in their willingness to have their attention directed by the stage magician.

The same method is employed in the pulp-fiction crime novel, known as the 'whodunit' novel, which employs the technique known as the 'red herring'. The red herring is a dubious character introduced at the beginning of the story with the intention of playing on the reader's natural desire to work out who the culprit it. The more confident the reader is that they know the red herring is the culprit, the less they will focus on the real culprit, who is often introduced a little later, and who will have the appearance of an insignificant character.

A third example of the mechanics of deception can be found in the confidence trick. A confidence trickster, or 'conman', will seek to gain a person's trust by doing them a favour. A simple example of this is for the conman to drop a small banknote on the floor in front of the victim and then ask them if it belongs to them. When the victim bends over to pick up the banknote, the conman will pull their wallet out of their back pocket. A more developed version of the confidence trick involves doing a favour for a stranger and then refusing any reward in return. This establishes a bond of trust, resulting in the victim seeing the conman as a 'decent person'. Once the image of a decent person has been established, it prevents the victim from scrutinising the real motives of the conman. Indeed, the purpose is to make the victim feel guilty about even suspecting the conman's motives at all. As with the other two examples, the aim is to control the attention of the person being deceived.

These examples of deception all tell us something about the difference between information and attention. What directs our attention is rarely the information itself, but our own emotions and motives, which are not open to scrutiny in the same way as the information presented. That is why emotions such as curiosity, suspicion and trust are employed for the purpose of manipulation. Logic can examine what is presented, but it cannot examine the motives behind what is presented, simply because these are indefinite, vague and hidden.

It is for this reason that military propaganda uses fear, suspicion and mistrust to engage the emotions of the general public, particularly during the run-up to war. The more forcefully an emotion such as anger or suspicion is felt, the more effective it will be at directing the attention towards the object of hatred. If we are convinced that someone is a traitor, or that another country is an enemy, then everything they do, even denial, will seem to confirm the fact.

What causes us to look beyond what is presented is the intuitive mind. When we first suspect that what is presented is not a complete picture, it is because we have been alerted by gut-feeling. This, however, will not tell us what is missing, or being hidden from us. In order to discover the hidden element, we have to hold off any immediate logical judgment until the less obvious elements come to the fore. These less obvious elements are always there, but the logical mind excludes them in order to focus on the more obvious elements of the situation. Logical thinking is about being 'right', and the more certain we are that we are right, the less we will be willing to admit that we might be wrong.

You work at a bank. You arrive at work on Monday morning to find out an enquiry is taking place. Money has gone missing and each member of staff is being called into the manager's office for questioning. You sit outside the manager's office waiting your turn, and you think about what happened before the weekend. You know you didn't take the money, but you know you will be a suspect because you were in the right time and place to steal it. You think about what you are going to say when you are asked about what you did on the day. You know that if you tell the truth and the real culprit is not found, you will be the prime suspect. And if you do not tell the truth and you are caught lying, you will look even guiltier. Would this alter your account in any way?

We assume that deception is something only dishonest people engage in. We associate deception with dishonesty, and if we want to be regarded as an honest person, we wouldn't engage in it. This view of deception comes from logic, which demands that something is either right or wrong, and so if we want to be good then we must avoid being bad. Because logical judgement is absolute, if we admit to any form of deception we will be branded as dishonest.

The problem is that life is much more complex than that. We have many thoughts and ideas which we dare not admit in public. We entertain romantic impulses and sexual fantasies, and if we admitted openly to such things we would be regarded as either immoral or possibly dangerous. And if we told our employer what we really thought of them we would not last long in employment. So, we hide such thoughts, and if we are asked directly about them, we either avoid answering them directly or deny them outright. It is for this reason that we have a public face and private thoughts.

Just as individuals have both an inner life and an outer life, the same can be said of institutions and organisations. A society will have closed meetings for its members, where they discuss private matters. A business will project a confident image in public, even if behind the scenes the reality is somewhat messier. The members of a government will haggle in private until a policy is agreed, and then claim to be united about the policy when it is presented to the public. There is a difference between what people say in private and what they do in public, and logic demands that if this difference is spotted, it must be condemned as deception or hypocrisy. Intuitively however we know there is a difference between a lie told to avoid embarrassment and a lie told to gain advantage.

If logical judgement is absolute, intuitive judgement is relative. Logic demands that if a person is caught telling a lie, they must be branded a 'lair'. Intuitively we know that even honest people can be dishonest on occasion and that dishonest people can come to regret their behaviour later. Intuitively we know that human nature is complex and contradictory and that human beings are fallible. So, while logic demands that a person must be labelled honest or dishonest, intuition takes the context, motives and circumstances of the person's actions into account.

Unless a person tells an obvious lie, we can rarely state with certainty that a deception is taking place. When we pick up on deception through gut-feeling, we can rarely say exactly what the deception is, merely that we feel there is something being hidden from us. We may pick up on a blush, an involuntary wince, the avoidance of eye contact or an odd tone of voice, and our gut-feeling will tell us there is something which is not being stated outright.

If the feeling persists, then we may have second thoughts about the hidden or unseen element. Such thoughts come from the intuitive mind. While logic focuses on the obvious, intuition picks up on the unobvious. We may hear a person speak, and we might reflect later on what they said and how they said it. It is this later reflection, which picks up on the anomalies or omissions, which alerts us to the deception. This later reflection is called hindsight, and hindsight is highly intuitive.

But perhaps it is the phenomenon of insight which is the most instructive in terms of deception. If deception is caused by a limited view of events, insight is the broadening of that view to include what was previously hidden from us. When we have an insight into another person's motives, for example, we may begin to see the situation from their point of view. Insight comes from trying to make sense of a gut-feeling that was there at the beginning, which alerted us to the hidden element, but we couldn't see what it was directly. An insightful thought will suddenly allow us to see what previously we couldn't see at all. Insight, like hindsight, is intuitive.

Good intuition does not mean we will never be deceived. Intuition is an ability, and it only becomes a skill through practice. If we do not attend to our intuitive ability, we may not hear our intuitive mind when it speaks. If we think logically, we will allow our convictions and prejudices to govern our thinking, and this can lead to adopting a limited view of what is presented. In order to think intuitively, we have to consider not just what is obvious but also what is unobvious. And what is unobvious doesn't jump out and announce itself to us. If we think we know what the truth is, we will not make an effort to look for what we presently do not know or cannot see. And what we do not know is often greater than what we know. We can be deceived because we accept a limited explanation or a limited view as truth. Sometimes we have to question what we call 'truth'.

Illusion

You meet a friend in the street. They look happy and you ask them why. They tell you they have a fear of spiders. They once woke up in the middle of night to find a spider on their bed and they haven't been able to sleep since. But now, they announce, they have found a solution. They pull a plastic lizard out of a bag and tell you that spiders are afraid of lizards, so they are going to put the plastic lizard on their bed to frighten the spiders away. Your friend looks happy and relaxed. You know that a spider wouldn't be able to see a plastic lizard in the dark, and so it wouldn't work. Would you tell them?

We assume that illusion is something which occurs only under special circumstances. We associate illusion with stage magic, clever graphics, mental illness or hallucinogenic drugs. For this reason, we do not associate illusion with everyday life. Because we regard illusion as an exception or a rare occurrence, we do not consider it important enough to give it more than a passing thought. But if by illusion we mean taking something at face value and without question, then illusion is much more common than is generally realised.

The words 'deception' and 'illusion' are often used in common, as though they mean the same thing, but there is a difference between them. Deception is a deliberate practice, while illusion is naive and unquestioning. A stage magician deceives the audience, while the audience enjoys the illusion of stage magic. A man who cheats on his wife deceives her, while his wife lives with the illusion of a happy marriage. In order to deceive we must have the intention of deceiving, but in order to live under an illusion we merely have to take what we see at face value or without question.

In order to see an illusion for what it is we have to be willing to question what we see, or at least the way we see it. This means looking again at what we take for granted and asking whether we see it as it is or whether we see only its most obvious features. William James (1842 - 1910), who wrote one the founding works on modern psychology, wrote, 'Note that in every illusion what is false is what is inferred, not what is immediately given'.

When we think logically, we attach a label to an experience. In order to do this, we have to simplify the experience and then attach a label to its most obvious feature; so, we may think of a flower in terms of its name, a dog in terms of its breed, or a person in terms of their skin-colour. This very simplified view of the world allows us to make quicker judgements but it has many disadvantages, the most obvious being that we see only what is included under the label.

Attaching a label to experience allows us to apply the 'is' or 'is not' judgement of logic. To demonstrate how this can distort our view of the world, it is useful to study the mechanics of illusion.

The mechanics of illusion can be studied most directly by the use of optical illusions. One of the most well-known examples of an optical illusion is the 'gestalt chalice', where the same image can be seen as either two profiles or a chalice between them. If we stare at the image for long enough, we will see how the mind interprets the illustration first as two profiles and then as a chalice, and then as two profiles again. The switching back and forth from one interpretation to another happens automatically, and without any intervention on our part. The image itself does not change, but the way the mind interprets the image changes. This happens because, when we are presented with a complex image, the mind reduces it until down to a single image so we can define it as one thing or the other.

The study of optical illusions tells us another thing about illusion; illusion is a product of the mind rather than the world around. An optical illusion does not trick the mind, but merely allows us to see the mind interacting with the illusion. What we are observing is the mind reducing a complex image down to one interpretation only. It is only because we can observe this that we marvel at the phenomenon of an optical illusion.

We might assume that once we look away from an optical illusion, the mind returns to its normal way of functioning, and we go back to seeing the world as it is. But it is the same mind, and the same functioning of the mind, that does this even when we are observing people and events in everyday life. If we are not aware of this, it is because under normal circumstances we don't notice it. The mind deals with all complex experiences in this way, and it is made more pronounced, rather than less, by the application of logic.

If we regard a person as good then we will find it difficult to see them as bad. If we regard something as a pleasure, we will find it difficult to see it as an indulgence. If a gambler believes they are lucky, they will ignore the number of times they have lost at gambling. If an addict believes they can beat their habit, it is usually because they have not yet tried. To see an illusion as an illusion we have to look at what we are missing, not what we are seeing. Logic will not allow us to accept contradictions, and so it forces us to defend one way of looking at the world and to reject anything which might contradict it.

This applies to all matters, great and small. It is the same mind we use to judge an individual, a nation or an epoch. If we believe the history of our country makes us great, then we will unable to see the darker elements of our history which contradict this. One of the ideals we live by, progress through technology, bears the hallmarks of a one-sided view of the world.

Technology has brought us mass-production and mass-destruction in equal measure.

We have attitudes, opinions and outlooks, and we like to think that our own outlook is the correct one and any outlook which differs from our own is wrong. Others also have their own attitudes, opinions and outlooks, and they also regard their own outlook as the correct one and regard all others who disagree with them as wrong. We cannot imagine that both sides can be partly right, partly wrong and partly limited in their outlook. Because we can't see this, we mistake our own outlook for truth. This means that what we often call 'truth' is not truth at all, but simply the illusion of truth.

You are walking through a busy train station on your way to work. You see a well-dressed man ahead of you, and he is handing out something to people who pass him by. You have seen this kind of thing before and you know it is usually sales leaflets or religious flyers. You try to avoid him but the station is busy; there are people hurrying on either side of you and so you are forced to walk directly past him. As you approach him you see he is holding a wad of banknotes. He smiles at you when he sees you and then hands one of the banknotes to you. Would you take it?

In order to see an illusion, we have to question what we see. If what we see appears to make sense then we will not question it. The occasions in life that cause us to question what we see are rare, and they usually involve an obvious illusion, such as when a person tries to portray themselves in an unconvincing manner. But illusion is much more common than is generally realised.

There are many illusions that are not regarded as such. For millennia people believed that the earth was at the centre of the universe and the sun revolved around it; indeed, if we take what we see at face value, that is how it appears. There was also a time when witches were blamed for crop failure. And there was even a period when a tulip bulb could be worth as much as a year's wages. We see such things as illusions because we have since questioned them.

While we are now free of the illusions of the past, illusion still plays a very important part in the modern world. We can see this, for example, in modern advertising. Advertising rarely sells the product, but more often sells the image associated with the product. Photographs of people with happy faces and confident smiles are intended to portray the image of what life would be like if we bought the product. We can also see the power of illusion in gambling, when the images on slot-machines convey riches and wealth rather than disappointment and loss. In the same way the images used to sell tobacco and alcohol are that of the romantic rebel rather than the penniless addict.

Such images are employed because they work, and they work because people are not driven by reason but by image and illusion. We buy a lottery ticket in the hope that our ticket, one amongst many millions, will be the winner. If we thought logically about this, we would not buy the ticket.

In addition to imagery in society, imagery also plays a part in the way we see other people. When we are falling in love, we see only the good side of the other person, and when we are falling out of love, we see only their faults. What we call a person's 'reputation' is very much the image they convey in public, rather than the complex reality of the actual person. It could be said that a uniform is an illusion; the uniform of the priest, the policeman and the judge all convey the image of assurance, and are intended to make us see the role rather than the person playing it. In the same way, the sex symbol, the confident salesman and the well-spoken politician are all a very much and image rather than reality.

Imagery is not logical or rational, but emotive, evocative and complex. This makes it difficult to apply logic or reason to deal with complex images. This applies not only to trivial matters but also to more complex and matters such as belief and ideals. Ideals such as progress, change and freedom contain much more imagination than reason, and many beliefs continue to exist in spite of the dominance of reason. The twentieth century has been portrayed as one of ongoing progress, and yet it gave us two world wars and two major revolutions.

We first become aware of the part played by illusion through gut-feeling. Gut-feeling will tell us not to trust an image, a uniform, a salesman's smile or an official account, even if it does not state in exact terms what the illusion is. Gut-feeling will also provide us with the first indications about any illusion we might have about ourselves. We might have the gut-feeling that we have been indulging too much, or that a clever remark was really a hurtful criticism, or that our expectations of life do not match the reality of our day to day existence. When our gut-feeling prompts us to think again, it is the first warning that we are seeing the whole picture. As with intuition applied to other problems, if we pay attention to our gut-feeling, further thoughts may come to provide more insight about what we are not seeing or attending to.

The problem with an illusion is that it can be pleasant and enjoyable; indeed, an illusory image must by nature be alluring otherwise we would scrutinise it for is flaws. That is why an addiction will seem pleasurable at first, and why free giveaways are offered to draw people into gambling online.

In spite of their unreal nature, illusions can be useful in life. It might be illusory to believe we can make the world a better place, but without it there would be no invention or art or ideology, or even any attempt at justice. We even need the illusion that we can make the world a better place to inspire our actions just as we need the illusion that we are going to find the perfect person in order to fall in love. Just because such things are illusory doesn't make them wrong or bad or even unattainable. The person who buys the winning lottery ticket does so under the same illusion as the millions who did not buy the winning lottery ticket.

The problem with illusion is not that it is unreal, but that we do not see it as such. If we buy a lottery ticket for fun, we will not be disappointed if we don't win. If we drink and know when to stop, we will not become an addict. The problem arises when we mistake the illusion for reality. If we fail to listen to our intuitive mind when it prompts us, we can entertain an illusion for many years before finally seeing it for what it is; then, when the hidden element finally reveals itself, we can become disillusioned. This is why illusion is a problem; once we see that the perfect lifestyle, the perfect person, or the perfect ideal is not perfect at all, what follows is not just disillusion but more often depression, and we have to live with that depression.

Enigmas

You are in a hospital ward with severe back pain.
The pain makes it difficult to sleep. You finally drop
off, but you are woken in the middle of the night
when the door opens and the lights come on. Two
security guards enter with an old woman on a
trolley. She is asleep and she looks heavily sedated.
They wheel the woman over to the bed next to you
and they lift her onto it. Then they handcuff the
woman to the bed. One of the security guards looks
at you and smiles reassuringly. Then the guards
walk back over to the door, switch off the lights and
leave. What are you thinking?

An enigma is a kind of puzzle or a problem. Whereas many enigmas are created for the purpose of entertainment, a genuine enigma is a naturally occurring one. If an enigma has been created as a kind of test, we can safely assume it will have an answer, but if the enigma is naturally occurring, there may be no obvious or direct answer to its solution.

Logic is the usual approach to problem solving. Logic demands that when we are confronted with an enigma, we try to gather as much information as possible, eliminate any misleading information and then process what remains until we arrive at the inevitable solution. The underlying assumption of this approach is that we have sufficient information to solve the problem. But when we do not have enough information, or when we are dealing with hidden information or with a limited view of the problem, then logic fails and we have to employ the intuitive method. Processing the available information will not solve a problem if not all the information is there.

A naturally occurring enigma exists because what we see does not make sense. It tells us there is something about what we are seeing which is hidden from us. It follows that if what we see does not make sense, then the fault lies with our understanding. Our knowledge of life is not based on what we see, but on what we understand. An enigma is something that defies our expectations, and that means our understanding of what is going on is limited.

We are surrounded by many more enigmas than we realise. Although we might assume if our understanding of the world was defective, it would be obvious to us, but it is not so. We can live with enigmas well enough; we do not have to know how a seed becomes a sheaf of wheat in order to bake bread. The dominance of logic means that we deal with the world in terms of definitions and labels, and so we make sense of an enigma by merely labelling it an 'enigma', an 'anomaly' or a 'puzzle' rather than getting to the root cause of the matter.

We can observe a falling apple, but we cannot observe the forces that cause the apple to fall. We can observe symmetry in a leaf, but we cannot observe the forces that cause the symmetry. We can see the geometric form in a pyrite crystal, but we cannot see the forces that cause the geometry. We can see vortexes in wind and water, but we cannot see the forces that cause the vortexes. And we can hear thunder roll, but we cannot see the forces that cause thunder to roll. If we take what we see at face value then we will never consider the forces behind what we see, and we will not notice an enigma even if it is right in front of us.

Isaac Newton was not the first to observe a falling apple; Galileo was not the first to observe a swinging pendulum, and Nikola Tesla was not the first to observe rolling thunder, but each was the first to regard the phenomenon as an enigma and then go on to think about what the cause might be. What makes an enigma an enigma is that we see it as such. And what causes us to see it as an enigma is the intuitive mind.

What first brings an enigma to our attention is gut-feeling; we feel that there is something more to what we see than meets the eye. If the gut-feeling persists, we may be tempted to apply logic to resolve the problem. This means that we try to explain the enigma in terms of what we already know. If this doesn't work, or if we are dissatisfied with the solution - and our gut-feeling tells us there is still more we do not see - then we may try to apply intuitive thinking. This means we must focus, not on what we know and see, but on what we are not yet seeing directly. This can lead to insight, when we suddenly see all that we saw before, but from a new and very different perspective. That is why new thoughts, new ideas and new insights are intuitive.

You are in a foreign country and you are walking along a dusty road. You see a large, vicious-looking dog by the side of the road, just ahead of you. As you approach the dog you see it is tied to a tree by a thick hemp rope. The dog has been chewing at the rope, but it stops when it sees you, and it looks at you and growls. You stop moving. The dog goes back to chewing the rope, and you watch it and wonder what will happen if it chews through it. You are trying to decide whether to pass by quickly before it chews through the rope when, with one last bite, the rope snaps and falls to the ground. The dog turns and looks at you again. It bares its teeth and growls but it doesn't move. What would you do?

There are some problems that can be solved logically and there are others that cannot be solved logically. Being able to say what an illness is does not provide us with a cure. Being able to say what causes unemployment does not create jobs. And being able to say that a dog is vicious does not tell us what to do next. Logic can tell us what 'is' or what 'is not', but it cannot tell us anything beyond that. What is more, when we are making a decision which has an unknown outcome, we have no way of knowing in advance whether we have made the right decision until after it has been made.

One of the greatest unknowns in life is the future; we can examine the past but we cannot examine the future. Our relationship with the future is very much like our relationship with an enigma; we know it is there, we can give it a name, but we cannot see it fully and so we can at best make guesses and assumptions about its nature. Because much of life is routine, we live with the assumption that we know the future. We make plans for the summer, decide on our choice of education, embark on projects to improve our home, and make new acquaintances in the hope they will bring us something good. All of this is sensible and right, but all of it is an assumption.

It is only when our routine is interrupted in some way that we are forced to consider the future as an unknown. It is then that we experience that nervous tension in the pit of the stomach known as 'gut-feeling'. Unless we understand why this happens, we will want to rid ourselves of this feeling as soon as possible. Nervous tension is uncomfortable, and we prefer to feel content. So, we look for answers and try to find the most plausible one, and try to settle on that. If the problem is relatively small, such as whether we will be reprimanded at work, or whether we will be late paying the rent, then we can wait until the uncertainty is resolved by events. But when it is a larger problem, such as whether we will be made unemployed, or whether an illness will affect us for life, then the gut-feeling will persist and cause us to reflect on our circumstances. That is why the bigger decisions in life are intuitive, because intuition deals with the unknown.

In order to train the mind to think intuitively we have to focus, not on what we know, but what we do not know. Enigmas provide very good exercises for thinking about the hidden or unknown elements of life. If we employ logic, we will treat an enigma as no more than a problem waiting for a name. If, however we employ intuition, we will regard an enigma as an opportunity to consider what we cannot yet see clearly or directly. For this reason, it is useful to consider enigmas as exercises to provoke the mind to consider what is hidden, unobvious and obscure. With an enigma, we know that there is more to what we see than meets the eye, and so we search for the hidden element within it.

Many of the traditional symbolic images are enigmatic. An image such as the Ouroboros, or the serpent biting its own tail, appears absurd and surreal at first sight. It could be said that the Ouroboros was created deliberately as an enigma. Many other traditional images, such as the Strength card of the Tarot, where a woman governs a lion, are examples of an obscure meaning. If we dismiss such images as nonsense, we will learn nothing from them. If, however we regard them as exercises in intuitive thinking, we will begin to see the meaning they intend to convey. Such images train the mind to think intuitively.

Because such images defy logic, they force us to consider what is inferred rather than what is stated openly. They perplex us and cause us to think in terms of what might be rather than what is. When the symbolic image is intentionally surreal, it is because what is being conveyed is indirect and complex. Its obscure nature prevents the mind from settling on one interpretation over another. That is why it is possible to interpret a symbolic image in more than one way.

Because the intuitive mind thinks in terms of images rather than fixed terms, it can explore complex imagery of this type without needing to reduce it down to a single interpretation. This allows the mind to remain fluid for much longer than logic would allow, and so makes room for new thoughts and new insights. New perspectives come through insight. Rather than applying an immediate label, the intuitive mind allows us to explore the image for its content, and to continue doing so until the meaning has been fully understood. With intuition, there is no right or wrong, but a gradual development of understanding through insight. This is particularly useful because, when we are considering the unknown or the hidden, many different perspectives are better than one.

In some respects, people are like symbolic images. We can observe the outer aspect of another person, but no more. We see them smile and deduce they are happy, but of course a smile can both convey happiness and disguise depression. We can know that our own emotions can be complex, our own inner life can be obscure, and our unconscious nature can be very mixed, and so it follows that other people must be the same. We know that we think one thing privately and say another publicly. If we are not quite as we appear, then it follows that others are not quite as they appear.

If we apply logic to our understanding of people then we will reduce this complexity down to a single label. Logic will judge a person by their uniform, job title or position in life, whereas intuitively we know that an ordinary worker can be as thoughtful, and even more so, than a government official. As with enigmas and symbolic images, understand people from many different perspectives is often better than one.

There are also enigmas in history. Any event can be seen from more than one point of view. Even in everyday life, from a domestic argument, to a traffic accident, to a dispute over a fence, there is often more than one side to a story. If we insist on seeing history from only one point of view, we will limit not just our understanding but also what we see. This means that we will reject any evidence which does not conform to our present understanding and accept only evidence that confirms it. What are called the enigmas of history are often examples when the orthodox account does not provide a satisfactory explanation to what happened. The more obvious enigmas of history include the identity of the Man in the Iron Mask, the personality of Saint Joan, the treatment of Kaspar Hauser, the origins of the French Revolution, and the assassination of the Archduke Ferdinand.

There are also enigmas which are not regarded as enigmas at all. We live with such enigmas because we have not stopped to question them. The proportions of the human body, the musical scale, symmetry in organic nature, and the synchronous rotation of the moon are all indications that we see only the outward aspect of a much more complex world. Time is an enigma, but we do not regard it as such. We see the movement of the hands on a clock and we do not consider why it is that we can see only the present. It is possible that time is exactly as it appears, but it is equally possible that we have a limited view of time. This limited view of time is rather like those who believed the world was flat because that was exactly how it appeared.

When the logical mind is dominant, the world is a closed book. For a logician, any problem has an answer, and the answer will be written in a book somewhere, and all we have to do is to find it. If the intuitive mind is dominant, the world is like a book we have not yet read, and we feel compelled to read it to find out what it can tell us. For the logical mind, an enigma is just a problem waiting for a solution. For the intuitive mind, an enigma is an indication that we do not see the world in its entirety, and that what we do see is only a small part of a much greater whole. If we don't see enigmas, it is because the logical mind is dominant, not because they don't exist.

The Outer World

You are a detective called to a crime scene. A woman has been found dead on the floor of her kitchen. You walk into the kitchen and see a blue table with four white chairs. There is a green mug on the table with red lipstick on the rim. On the table, next to the mug, is a passport, a plane ticket and a cream handbag. The handbag is open. You look inside and see a brown purse and a set of car keys. You look at the woman lying on the floor; she is wearing a cream floral dress and red stilettoes. She does not seem to have been assaulted. You notice there are traces of blood around her mouth. Then it occurs to you that the lipstick on the mug was actually blood. Without reading the above paragraph again, what was the colour of the mug?

We can live well enough without attending to the world around. We can walk through a park and not really notice the flowers, or hear someone speak and not really listen to what they are saying, or eat a meal and not really taste the flavour. We can do all of this and live well enough to catch the morning train, read an email and eat a sandwich at lunchtime. This form of living, living without really attending to life, is sometimes referred to as being on 'autopilot', or behaving like a machine operating without human control.

We spend much of our time on 'autopilot' and, in some respects, the ability to act and think mechanically is useful. We can write down a telephone number without paying attention to what our hand is doing. We can drive a car without paying attention to what our feet are doing. We can type a letter, brush our teeth, or stop at a red light while thinking about something else entirely. Mechanical actions of this type are the result of repeated behaviour, and it this both necessary and useful in life.

Equally, mechanical behaviour can also be problematic or even dangerous. If we try to put a stop to a habit such as nail-biting, we may find ourselves absentmindedly biting our nails again. We may find ourselves coming off a motorway into a built-up neighbourhood and then suddenly realise we are still driving at high speed. And we might respond violently to a provocation, only to discover later the provocation was deliberately intended to produce that result. The question is not whether the action is mechanical, but whether we can attend to it, and therefore intervene, when we need to.

In the same way that we have mechanical habits, we can also think mechanically. Many of our prejudices and unchecked assumptions are the product of mechanical thinking. It can even be said that mechanical thinking and mechanical behaviour go hand in hand. So, when we do not attend to the outer world, it is probably because our thinking is governed by habit, assumption or logic

The problem is not that we can act and think mechanically, but that we do it unconsciously. In order to become aware of this, and to be able to keep this aspect of our behaviour in check, we have to employ intuition. Intuition is the watching mind; it watches over us as we think and speak and act. When we listen carefully to what a person says, because we are trying to understand them, or when we read a book attentively, because we are looking for specific information, or when we walk through a park and look for the first signs of spring, we do so with the active attention of the intuitive mind.

When we listen without really hearing, or look without really seeing, it is because the intuitive mind is passive. That is why an intuitive thought can cause us to look again at what we had previously overlooked. When we notice a change in the breeze and it occurs to us that winter is coming, or when we observe a cat and wonder about what is going on in their mind, or when we witness a new social movement and wonder what are the causes behind it, it is because the intuitive mind is active. Intuitive thoughts prompt us to look again at what we might otherwise take for granted. This is why intuitive thoughts often seem to come out of the blue; the intuitive mind is prompting us to attend to the hidden behind the visible outer world.

We do not just look with the eyes and hear with the ears. If we simply observed the world around, we would remember very little of what we saw or heard, and we would understand even less. In order to remember what we have seen or what we have heard we have to attend to it intuitively. This is not the same as analysis; when it is said we shouldn't 'over-think', it means we shouldn't try to analyse our actions as we perform them. Intuition is about attending to our actions rather than analysing them.

If we attach labels to the most obvious features of our experience, we will not attend to anything that falls outside that label. We may walk through a park, pass by other people and look up to the sky for rain, but if we think only in terms of labels - 'park', 'person' or 'sky' – then we will be unlikely to look beyond the label. The intuitive mind will pick up on the first falling leaves, the tension in a person's footsteps, or the scent of damp in the air, and it will prompt us to look beyond the label.

The intuitive mind is always there, always watching, but if we do not pay attention to it, we will act and think and speak on 'autopilot', and we may do this for a whole day, or longer, without noticing it.

Imagine you are standing at the top of your local High Street (this is best done when the street is not in view). Now imagine the first shop or business at the top of the High Street, and think of the name of it. Then imagine you are walking down the High Street, and mentally name each shop as you pass it. If you are honest you will find that you can name less than half of the shops on the High Street, even though you might have walked past them a hundred times.

In order to actively observe the world around, as distinct from passively looking at it, we have to attach a thought or a word to what we observe. When we see a flower, we think 'flower', and when we see an apple, we think 'apple'. In the above test, you will find that the businesses you can remember are those that you have had an active interest in, rather than the ones you have simply passed by as you walked along the High Street. In order to observe the outer world with attention, we also have to attend to the inner world of our thoughts.

Because we attend to what we see with a thought, the richness of what we see outwardly depends on the richness of what we think inwardly. If we think of the world in simple terms, we will see the world in simple terms. If we think we see the world rightly, it is because we see it logically, and that means to draw from a very limited perspective. A child, a farmer and an artist will all look at the same lamb, but see the lamb from their own perspective. An investor and an artist will both look at the same work of art, but they will see the same work of art from a different perspective.

One of the most difficult things to pay attention to is what is not clear, apparent or obvious in a situation. We may criticise a person's choice of clothing because we see the clothing, but we cannot see their reasons for making the choice. We may see someone display a sudden outburst of anger, but we will be unable to see the hidden causes that led up to the outburst. These hidden or unobvious elements will not come to the fore if our thinking is dominated by logic. If we can hold off an immediate right or wrong judgment, then gut-feeling, second thoughts and intuitive insights can emerge to provide us with a fuller perspective.

The secondary elements of an experience can often be more revealing than the more obvious aspects. There is a difference between a real smile and a forced one, a genuine outburst of anger and an act, or a heartfelt compliment and mere flattery. When we pick up on these secondary aspects, it is because the intuitive mind is drawing our attention to what is not obvious and apparent. The intuitive mind can detect the difference between a careless remark and one intended to hurt. It can tell the difference between an enjoyment and an indulgence, or a spontaneous act and a premeditated one.

When the intuitive mind first draws our attention to the hidden elements in a situation, it is usually through gut-feeling. Gut-feeling can appear vague and imprecise, but this is because it is picking up on the vague and imprecise elements of the situation. Gut-feeling will not tell us what the hidden is, only that it is there; to know what the hidden element is, we have to wait for insight. So, we may hear tension in a person's voice but not be able to say why it is there.

Later, after some reflection, we may remember a long-forgotten disagreement with that person, and suddenly understand what the cause of the tension was. We may hear the account of a public event and feel that something in the account is missing, but may not be able to say what it is. Then after some time, and with the arrival of new information, we may have some insight into the missing element. We may even have the feeling we are being observed, and not be able to make anything more of it than that, only later to discover that we were indeed being observed.

Gut-feeling picks up on many things which cannot be defined logically or clearly, because what it picks up on is often not logical or clear. If we wait and watch and keep an open mind, insights may follow which can be more informative than any snap judgement we made at the time. The intuitive mind is much slower than the logical mind because second thoughts take time to arrive.

The same approach can also help us to understand events in the wider world. A change can occur in the political mood of a country and, when it does, the appointed authorities are often the last to recognise it. The phrase 'war drums' is sometimes used to indicate an unconscious aggression which often leads to conflict. We pick up on such things through gut-feeling, and then insight provides the secondary thoughts that can help us to make sense of it.

What we think affects not just what we see, but how we respond to what we see. The dominance of logic means that not only do we see the world in terms of black and white, but that we deal with the world in terms of black and white. This is why strong opinions and ideological arguments, from religion to politics, to science and economics, are often conducted in fierce and combative terms. If we see the world in terms of an exclusive ideology, then we will be forced to take sides and to portray one side as right and the other as wrong, or possibly even dangerous. It is often from this approach that conflict arises.

It follows that a richer and more varied thought-life will lead to a richer and more varied understanding of the outer world. If we hear an opinion different from our own, we can react negatively to it. If we spot an enigma, we can dismiss it as a mere anomaly. If we hear an account or an explanation which does not quite add up, we can point to the inconsistencies and reject it on that basis. Or we can pick up on such things intuitively. We can listen to a person speak and try to gain insight into what their motives might be. We can walk through a park and try to pick up on the mood of nature. We can observe a political event and ask ourselves what is behind it. To be able to see more outwardly, we have to see more inwardly, and that means to engage the watching mind.

An active intuition can lead to a more developed understanding of the world around; to people, nature, events, and even ourselves. A walk along a High Street can be a dull and routine experience or it can be a highly fascinating one. A simple meal can be a necessity or it can be an enjoyable feast. And we can regard a lifetime as a disappointment or as an adventure; it all depends on how we see it. Fascination, interest and enjoyment all come from the intuitive mind, and are not automatic properties of the outer world.

People-Watching

A member of your family has recently admitted to a gambling addiction. They managed to hide it for years by lying about their losses. They claimed they were burgled, mugged, and then dismissed from work unfairly. You and your family came to their aid and helped them out financially. Eventually the stories became unbelievable and they were forced to admit the addiction. Now they are in your home and asking you for help. They say they cannot pay their rent and are about to be evicted. They fear they will become homeless and destitute and never recover. They tell you it was humiliating to admit their gambling addiction but now they are facing up to it and they just need a bit of help. They beg you for money to pay the rent. What would you do?

Of all the unknowns in life, people provide the most obvious example of what is hidden from direct observation. Of course, we can observe their appearance and mannerisms, and we can deduce much from that, but the most essential nature of the individual – what is going on inside – is not open to direct scrutiny. Other unknowns, such as the laws of nature or the future, might concern us from time to time but we cannot ignore people. Our interactions with other people take up so much of everyday life that we cannot defer judgement until we have enough information to decide how to deal with them on a rational basis, so we have to make an intuitive judgement about them.

We spend much of our time trying to work out what other people think, what they want, how they feel and how they will react if we have to have any dealings with them. We want to know whether they like us or not, whether they respect us or not and - perhaps most crucially - whether we can trust them or not. And we need to know this because we see only the outer aspect of people, not the inner life; the inner life is hidden.

In some respects, it could be said that people are as much an enigma as the enigmas of nature or time. What is more, nature does not actively deceive us. If a stone falls to the ground, then gravity is the cause, and if an apple looks rotten, then it is rotten. But human beings are not so direct. A person can smile when they are unhappy, express anger when they are not, and hide their intentions and say what they do not really believe in order to gain an advantage over us. Perhaps that is why many people prefer the company of animals; if a dog wants to chase a ball, we do not have to ask why.

Because logic is dominant in society, logic is also the dominant approach to understanding human nature. We define people in terms of race, gender, class, sexuality, education, vocation, politics or religion, and we do so because we believe this will tell us something about what they are like inside. The problem with this approach is twofold; firstly, it greatly simplifies human nature, and secondly it demands that human beings are consistent, and any experience of life will tell us they are not. Pleasant people can become angry and aggressive under pressure, and aggressive people can be very well-behaved in the company of their parents. Logic reduces people down to single, identifiable labels, but our own observation of people will tell us that people are far more complex than can be defined by a single label.

When we observe people through the eyes of logic, we see either a politician, police officer, a doctor, a pensioner, a scientist or a priest. When we view people in terms of labels, we do not see individuals. If we define a group of men as white and middle class, we assume that all white, middle class men are the same; that they see the world through the same eyes, and remain the same throughout life. But few people go through life without undergoing some kind of change in their outlook, and what we want in old age is not the same as what we wanted when we were young.

Most of all logic fails to help us to understand people because people are not logical; indeed, it could be said that it is our unwillingness to conform to any label or stereotype that makes us most human.

The intuitive method adopts a different approach to people-watching. Whereas logic sees people in terms of definitions and labels, intuition sees people in terms of emotions, images and complexity. Intuitively we know that people have complex personalities, mixed views and inconsistent beliefs. People can be rational at times, emotional at times, and indifferent at times. Atheists can become converts, and religious people can lose their faith. Logical judgement is absolute, but intuitive judgement is relative and conditional. People are only consistent some of the time.

Intuition is slower than logic when it comes to forming judgements, and because of this, the intuitive approach is more suited to understanding human nature. Many of the features of the human character are not obvious or open to direct inspection, which is why it can take many years to actually get to know someone. We can detect the more obvious features of a person, such as laziness or aggression, but the less obvious features such as a hidden bitterness or a harboured grudge can be more difficult to observe. This is why we pick up on such things intuitively. We may see an involuntary wince, or a flash of the eyes, or hear a tension in a person's voice, and begin to wonder what is the cause of it. What we see depends on what we think, and the richer our inner life, the richer will be our observation of other people.

We can watch others passively, just as we can be passive observers on a train, or we can watch them actively, as a bird-watcher observes the mating dance of a bird. If we want to understand other people, we have to watch them actively; and if we want to watch them actively, then we have to do it intuitively.

You walk into a pub and you see an old friend at the bar. You go across to join him and he tells you he is waiting for his date to turn up. You tell him you thought he was already in a relationship; he says that he is, but he is unhappy in it, and so he is looking for someone new. Then he tells you he joined a dating website under a false name so his partner wouldn't know. He says he has met four women this way in the last month. The date arrives and she joins you at the bar. She is pretty and naive and she engages both of you in conversation. You are careful not to betray your friend. Then your friend goes to the toilet and you are left alone with the date. She asks you what kind of person your friend is. What would you say?

Any attempt to understand people must contend with the fact that people will reveal in public only a small part of what is going on inside. Indeed, people will take active steps to prevent anyone from scrutinising their inner life too closely. This secrecy is not an aberration or an exception in human nature, but a fact of life.

A little self-knowledge will tell us there is much we do not like to admit to others or to say in public. We have personal secrets; there are things we are embarrassed about - petty fears, harboured grudges, personal criticisms, fantasies and sexual desires - and for the most part we prefer to keep such things to ourselves. If we admitted such things in public we would be regarded as either not quite right or possibly even dangerous. So, we keep such thoughts to ourselves. If we can accept that we do not express such thoughts in public, then it is not too difficult to accept that others do the same.

And yet there is something more about the inner life than the elements we do not reveal to others; there are also many things we will not admit even to ourselves. Just as we are ashamed to admit our vanities and jealousies to others, we also find it difficult to admit such things to ourselves. We find it difficult to admit that we crave another's approval, or that another person's criticisms do actually hurt, or that we can be motivated by jealousy or revenge. We do not like to admit such things to ourselves because they belittle us. This means there is an element of our inner life which is not obvious and open, even to ourselves. It is for this reason that we cannot understand other people simply by asking them direct questions; we cannot ask them what they think if they are not even being honest with themselves about what they think.

Simple labels do not help us to understand the complexity of human nature, and if we want to observe people in order to understand them as distinct from merely passing judgement on them, we have to observe them intuitively. The way to do this is to prevent our own prejudices, which come from the logical mind, from interfering with our observations. If we can do this, the secondary or less obvious elements of a person's character will come to our attention. And it is often the secondary or less obvious elements of a person's character which are most revealing.

We pick up on these secondary elements in another person's character by observing the smaller, involuntary acts which often betray their more public face. A wince, a frown, a fidget or a hesitation can often tell us more than a dozen direct questions. In order to be able to pick up on involuntary actions of this type, we have to be fluid enough in our thinking to pick up on them, and broad enough in our understanding to make sense of them. The harsh judgements of logic cannot do this.

The intuitive method regards people as enigmas. In the same way an enigma can be perplexing and confusing, people can be perplexing and confusing. The unwillingness of the intuitive mind to settle on a single judgement is not a disadvantage when it comes to people-watching, but is actually more suited to human nature. Just as a symbolic image can have many layers of meaning, so too with human nature. There is, for example, what can be observed outwardly, then what a person chooses to keep hidden, and then what a person hides even from themselves. All of this takes time to understand, and we understand it best by holding off our logical judgements and waiting for the intuitive mind to provide us with the insight into each of the elements. Just as our understanding of ourselves is progressive, our understanding of others is the same. We can sometimes be surprised to discover that a close friend does not actually like us, or that a person we have never regarded as a friend does in fact like us.

We have no choice but to make character judgements about people. We do this because what we see and hear is only one aspect of a much more complex inner life. People can be evasive, secretive and emotional; they can say one thing and mean another; they can be genuinely offended or feign offence, and they can lie convincingly or even tell the truth unconvincingly. All of this can be observed through quiet observation, and quiet observation is the hallmark of the intuitive mind. Perhaps most of all what makes for good character judgements about others is a degree of honesty about ourselves, and this too is intuitive.

The better our intuition, the better will be our ability to read other people. People-watching can be a passive activity or the means to understand human nature, but only if the intuitive mind is engaged in the exercise. Just as we can eat a meal without really tasting it, we can spend a lifetime in the company of others and never really understand them. There are many useful skills in life, and there is a formal education for most of them, but perhaps the most useful skill in life is to be able to read others rightly. People are a constant reminder that we see too little and know too little.

If we want to observe people intuitively, we have to observe silently. People often reveal more in a wince than in any carefully prepared statement. A wince cannot be labelled or defined, and yet it can be a very real expression of what is going on inside. The same can be said for a tone of voice, tension in a face, the narrowing of the eyes, a nervous smile, and so on. What gives such things meaning is the wider context in which they occur, which is why logic deals badly with people-watching.

The more deliberate our people-watching, the more we will become aware that the intuitive mind provides us with insights as we observe. It could be said that life provides us with no greater enigma than human nature.

Decisions

You are applying for a job. You arrive outside the interview room and you see a former colleague who is applying for the same job. You sit next to them and wait. While you are waiting, you admit to your former colleague that you are worried you don't have all the necessary qualifications. He looks at you and smiles knowingly, and then tells you that they only check the qualifications if they have reason to suspect them. You are called into the interview room and you answer all the questions confidently. The people who interview you all seem positive towards you. They tell you they will let you know by the end of the week. At the end of the week you receive an email telling you they were impressed by you, but unfortunately the job went to someone who was more qualified. What would you do?

Our important decisions usually involve thinking about the future. Whether the decision is about a job, a home or a person, what we are trying to resolve is how our actions will work out in the future. The problem with the future is that we cannot see it directly, and so we have to guess what the outcome will be. The more guesswork, the more uncertainty there will be about whether the decision is the right one or not. When this happens, we experience the kind of anxiety in the pit of the stomach that we call 'gut-feeling'. Logic allows us to focus on the elements of the decision we are certain about, such as the facts, details and observable elements involved, but gut-feeling draws our attention to the elements of the decision we are not certain about, such as the possible outcomes, the intentions of others and our own unchecked motives.

Making a decision about an unknown future is like walking into a darkened room; we much prefer to have the light on. The aim of thinking, particularly when it is employed in decision-making, is to throw light on what we presently cannot see directly. Self-observation will tell us we employ both logic and intuition to this end, and more-often we begin by trying to apply logic.

We use logic to make day-to-day decisions because, for the most part, day-to-day decisions are about lesser matters such as whether we like curry or not, or whether our income exceeds our outgoings. Much of life is routine; we wake in the morning, wash and dress, go to work, perform our duties, head for home, eat a meal and then retire for the night. All of this allows us to assume we live in a world we know and understand well enough. We only have to think about the unknown when our day-to-day routine is in some way interrupted. It is when this happens, for example when we are faced with unemployment or eviction or a divorce, that we feel the unknown directly.

The bigger decisions in life are regarded as such because they are usually irreversible. Such decisions can include moving to a new home, choosing a career, finding a partner or ending a relationship. It is when the decision is life-changing that we feel this unknown element most directly, and not logically, but emotionally.

Because our greater decisions in life are emotional, it is the emotional element which is the most important part of the decision. While we can consider the price and location of a new home, or think about the prospects of a new career, or take compatibility into account when finding a new partner, ultimately it is the emotional impact of the decision which matters most. This is because we have to live with the consequence of the decision, and living with it means living with it emotionally.

That is why logic is insufficient for dealing with the bigger decisions in life, because our emotions are not logical. We can feel hopeful and fearful at the same time; we can wish we didn't have to make an important decision and yet still feel relieved at finally having to make it, and we can resent someone for hurting us and still care deeply about them. If the major decisions in life often seem mixed and confused, it is because our emotional life is often mixed and confused.

Even a decision which seems to affect only the outer world will have its correlation with the inner life. A new home may be closer to work but it may mean moving away from our friends or family. A career choice may be a good source of income but it may be dull and uninteresting. A divorce may be messy and full of turmoil, but continuing in an unhappy relationship might be even more unpleasant. Distinguishing between what is outer world and what is inner life may not be possible, and for that reason, most decisions of this type are a balanced judgement. If we use a 'tick box' approach to this type of decision making, we may find ourselves left with feeling that something is still left out of the decision. This missing element is often what cannot be defined logically or pinned down with an exact phrase or statement.

If we were machines, we could make logical judgments and live with the consequences. But we are not machines, and so in order to make our more important decisions, we have to get in touch with that part of our inner life which does not subject well to logic. The logical mind cannot do this, but the intuitive mind can.

You run a business and it is failing. The auditors are due in the morning, and you know that when they see the books, they will shut you down. You have a mortgage and you know you will lose your home as well as your business. You have not told your friends or family about how bad the situation is, and you will find it very humiliating to do so. You have until

the morning to decide what to do. You could hide
your losses, but if you are caught you would be
charged with fraud. You could take out a short-term
loan but you would only end up in even more debt.
You could also take whatever cash and valuables you
have and leave town, but even if you were not caught
you would never be able to return home. Or you
could be honest and lose your business, your home
and your reputation. What would you do?

Because logic forces us to think in terms of right and wrong, it means that when we are confronted with complex situations, we feel compelled to choose between one action and another. From the point of view of logic, if we cannot decide is it because we are muddle-headed and unable to think clearly. But the inability to decide may be no more than the recognition that the situation is complex and there are no obvious right or wrong choices. Indeed, the inability to decide may be the intuitive mind calling us to consider the wider picture before we act.

From the point of view of logic, intuitive thinking is emotional, and therefore fuzzy and imprecise. And yet the emotions are just as real as money and jobs and payments, and even though we cannot grasp them with our hands or see them with our eyes, they affect everything we do, and play a particularly important part in decision-making. Logic demands that we exclude our emotions, dreams, fears and desires from the decision-making process, and then come to a sensible and rational conclusion about which is the best action to take. The problem with this is that while our hopes and fears may be unfounded, they have a very real effect on what we think and do; fear does not have to be real to be felt as real.

In addition to the emotions, our more important decisions are also affected by our image of ourselves. We do not just start up a business for money, but for what the money will bring. We do not just marry to produce children, but for the image of what married life will bring. This kind of imagery plays a part in our decision making, but it is often hidden and remains in the background of our more rational thinking because images of this type cannot be defined in the way the legality of an action can be defined.

Rather than ignore this messier aspect of our inner life, the intuitive mind acknowledges it for what it is. The intuitive approach is to see and observe rather than to judge. The more we see, the more informed we will be when it comes to making the final decision. Logic wants us to think in terms of right versus wrong and this means anything improper, unacceptable or imperfect has to be ignored or excluded from the final decision. When we do this, we divide our inner life into right and wrong, and only allow ourselves to think about what is right, no matter how much the hidden elements influence the final decision.

If we try to exclude our emotions, desires or fantasies from the decision-making process, we may find ourselves with a feeling of inadequacy about the decision we have made. The intuitive approach however does not divide our emotions, desires and fantasies into real and unreal, it simply acknowledges that they exist.

We experience gut-feeling as the form of anxiety felt the pit of the stomach. This can be unpleasant, particularly if we are faced with a decision that requires immediate action. Gut-feeling will tell us there is something we cannot see clearly, but it will not always tell us what it is. So, we may feel that something is missing or overlooked, but no be able to say what it is exactly. Nonetheless, if we allow ourselves to accept this feeling, then we can begin to look for what the missing element might be.

The intuitive method is much slower to judgment than the logical method. This is a reflection of the way the intuitive mind works. In order to see with the mind, we have to be inclusive and open-minded rather than narrow-minded and blinkered. The slower judgement of the intuitive mind is an outcome of taking in more information before making a decision. So rather than try to sort out our complex emotions, the intuitive mind accepts them as complex. The anxiety that we associate with gut-feeling comes from not being able to see the problem fully, and not being able to see the outcome at all, coupled with the fear that we may not be able to reverse any decision we might make.

If we continue to observe before coming to a judgement – provided the situation will allow - then what was once unclear will become clearer over time. If we observe in this way, we may have insights into the hidden element, when we suddenly see what we could not have seen previously. Insight provides a wholly new and different perspective on the situation. This can happen suddenly and unexpectedly; it is for this reason an insightful thought is usually described as a flash of light or a bright idea.

The worst decisions we make in life are usually those that have been made for the wrong reasons. If we have examined our motives honestly and thought about the situation clearly, then any decision we make will be, at the very least, based on a full understanding of our motives for making it. This does not mean that the decision will be the right one, but simply that it will be an honest one. If we are honest with ourselves about why we are making a decision, then at least we will be able to live with the outcome even if it is not quite as we imagined it would be.

It is not that we must choose between intuitive or logical thinking in order to make a decision, but simply that we can use both. If we apply hard and fast logic too early in the decision-making process, we will get a very limited view of both the situation and our inner thoughts and feelings. Our initial response to any experience is intuitive, and this is particularly true with respect to new and unknown situations. The intuitive approach recognises this and allows us to consider the different elements in a situation, even though they may be contradictory or confusing. Rather than eliminate these intuitive responses at the outset, it may be better to allow them to inform our thinking so that we arrive at a fuller view of the problem over time.

When we are about to make a decision and we have the gut-feeling that something isn't right, it is because the intuitive mind is trying to tell us that we are missing something very important. The phenomenon of hindsight can often reveal what we did not pay attention to at the time. That is why we can sometimes look back on our past actions with regret. The better informed we are about why we are making a decision, the less likely we will regret the decision.

Judgements

A blind man lives locally and you get to know him over many years. He is cheerful and likeable and you stop to chat with him whenever you see him. You are walking along a street with a friend when you see the blind man up ahead and so you stop and say 'hello'. The blind man invites you and your friend back to his house for a drink, and you both decide to go along. He offers you both a beer, and he is clearly enjoying the company. Then you see your friend take an item from the blind man's side-cabinet and put it in his pocket. Your friend looks at you and smiles knowingly. What would you do?

A judgement is not the same as a decision. We can make a judgement about a person, a group, an idea or an event and not feel the need to act on it in any way. A decision usually leads to an action, but a judgement is an inner attitude. It could be said that we make ongoing judgements and occasional decisions.

Logic plays an important part in the decision-making process because any decision usually involves choosing between one alternative or another. If you are driving along a road and you come to a junction, you have to decide whether you are going to turn right or left. You can consider the items on a menu, but eventually you must choose between one or another item. And if there is a war and you are called to fight, you must decide what to do, quite apart from your judgement about the motives for the war.

Because we do not have to act on a judgment, judgements do not have to be absolute. We can enjoy the company of a friend but not wholly trust them. We can work happily with others but not want to socialise with them. We can agree in part with an opinion without having to agree with all of it. Because a judgement does not have to lead to a specific action, it can be broad, balanced and conditional. We can be content with our life and yet still grumble about it.

A judgement arises from thinking about what we observe. We do not simply observe the world around, we attach a thought or an idea to what we observe. We see the sun rise, or hear a dog bark, and we attach a label to the experience. And yet thinking is more than simply attaching a label to an experience; in order to make sense of the world we have to connect one experience with another to form an attitude, an outlook or an opinion. We see the sun rise one morning, and then again, the next morning, and from this we conclude that it must rise again the next day. We then use the word 'sunrise' to describe that set of experiences. If one stray dog barks at us, and then another does the same, we will form a judgement or an opinion about stray dogs. A judgement is an overview or an inner attitude to what we experience.

Because logic demands that we think in terms of 'is' or 'is not', it forces us into one-sided judgements. If logic is dominant in our thinking, we will feel compelled to decide whether a person is good or bad, or whether a religion is true or false, or whether a politician is honest or dishonest. From the point of view of logic, if we cannot decide one way or the other then we are being woolly-minded or confused. Logic will not allow us to accept that a person can have a mixture of good and bad qualities, or that a religion may be based on part-truth and part-falsehood, or that a politician can be honest most of the time but lie occasionally. And yet we know that many people, societies and cultures often display just such a mixture of qualities. Intuitively we can accept this, and so our unwillingness to come to a harsh judgement does not necessarily mean we are indecisive, but merely that intuitively we accept the situation for what it is.

Many of our judgements come ready-made from life. We are born into a society where there are developed attitudes about religion, politics, economics, morality, justice and law. The dominance of logic means that many of our ready-made judgements are often one-sided and biased. This is most obvious in politics, where an election will force us to choose between one political party or another. It can also be seen in formal religion, where we must choose between one religion or another, or even in the rejection of religion altogether. The dominance of logic in society means that we adopt many absolute judgements and attitudes even before we have thought about them.

It is only when we begin to think independently, when we begin to question the absolute values provided by society, that we begin to apply intuitive thinking. We can vote for the party of our choice and still have our reservations about them. We can dislike religion but still believe in a deity. And we can acknowledge that a person can be guilty of a crime and yet still be a human being and capable of reform. So, while many of the logical judgements we inherit are absolute, our own intuitive judgements often relative.

The advantage of being relative in our judgements is that we can go on forming them over many years. We can modify our judgements depending on how much we understand, how much information we have, and whether the broader context has changed or not. We can then consider new information in its own right without having to accept or reject it on the basis of whether it agrees with our existing judgement. An honest person may go through a bad patch, and a rogue may come to regret their behaviour later in life. A society can go from being religious to being secular, and then go back to being religious again. The political mood of a country can change from being right-wing to left-wing, or from liberal to authoritarian, and then back again. If we think intuitively, we can detect such changes without the need to attack or defend one viewpoint over another.

Perhaps the area where intuitive judgement is most necessary is in our judgement of other people. The black and white judgement of logic means that we must see a person as either good or bad. It means that if a person is caught lying or stealing, they can be tarnished for life, even if the lie or the theft was small. This can lead to a highly intolerant view of others, and one based on a past judgement rather than on present behaviour. Intuitive judgement is more suited to human nature because people are not always rational or consistent, few people are wholly good or bad, and anyone can go through a bad patch. Only a machine is consistent.

You are a prisoner in a war; you are also the senior officer in the prison camp. One of the guards has discovered a knife hidden behind the latrine. The commander of the camp has ordered all the prisoners to line up in the yard. He demands to know who put the knife there, and he orders you, as the senior officer, to tell him who it was. You know who put it there but you do not want to betray them, so you put yourself forward as the culprit. The commander asks you what type of knife it was, and when it becomes obvious you don't know, they demand that you turn over the real culprit. You remain silent. The commander then says that if you do not turn the real culprit over to them, they will take each prisoner in turn and have them beaten until one of them reveals who it was. What would you do?

Most judgements occur within a particular context. What makes something right or wrong is often the context in which the judgement is made. A good joke at a wedding may be a bad joke at a funeral, and being drunk at midnight is acceptable but being drunk at midday is not. What makes something good or bad is largely the context in which it occurs.

Logic cannot deal with contexts because contexts are relative. A context is the coming together of many lesser elements to create a very real set of circumstances. If we are in a theatre and everyone is laughing, we will feel like laughing too. If there is an election and everyone is discussing politics, we will be tempted to discuss politics. What creates a context is not a single element but a combination of them. A quiet restaurant may be relaxing, while a busy restaurant may have a vibe. Logic deals badly with contexts because they are not singular and definable, and therefore difficult to label.

We only notice the environment when it changes suddenly, such as when the weather drops, or when a neighbour turns up their music, or when we find ourselves caught in a hostile crowd. If we are accustomed to the environment, we will cease to notice it, such as when we live next to railway tracks, or in a continually hot climate, or when violence is commonplace. We are always operating within a context, but we rarely notice it. Asking someone to consider the context they operate in is like asking a fish to consider the water it swims in.

We pick up on the influence of a context intuitively, through gut-feeling. Gut-feeling will tell us there is something we cannot see directly, and that we have to pay attention to it. When there is a change of mood at a dinner party, or when someone speaks in a loud voice in a library, or when we enter a city park and suddenly notice the calm mood, it is because our gut-feeling has picked up on the context around us.

There are formal contexts, such as a day job, or a marriage, or a school room. When the context is formal, we can use logic to help us make a judgement about what is right and wrong. If an employee is late for work, or a partner has an affair, or a student is unruly, we can judge the action from within the given context. Contexts become formal by being fixed over time, which makes them possible to define. Football or soccer began as a very primitive sport and has now evolved into a highly complex game, full of rules and exceptions and its own culture of terms, set-pieces and defined strategies.

Many contexts are not formal, and their very nature makes them difficult to fix and define precisely. Such contexts cannot be labelled in the way a formal context can, but nonetheless they are just as real in terms of their impact on our judgement and behaviour. An informal context can be a group of friends on a night out, the momentary excitement of a group of schoolchildren, or the negativity that follows immediately after a broken affair. Logic cannot deal with informal contexts of this type because they are dependent on circumstances, people and occasion. The same group of friends can be rowdy on one night and well-behaved the next, and no amount of logic can be used to predict such behaviour.

We are not normally aware of the context we operate in, largely because we are inside it. A context is like our own accent; we only hear it when we are in the company of others with a different accent. The context of fashion is highly instructive in this regard; what appears normal to one generation will appear as either absurd or embarrassing to the next. If we are not aware of the effect of a context on our actions it is because we cannot see it, not because it doesn't exist. At one time it would have been absurd to suggest the world was governed by atoms; now it is absurd to suggest that it is not.

When we make a judgement, whether it is about a person, an event or an idea, it is within a given context. If we live in times of prosperity, we may decide to start up a new business. If we live in times of uncertainty we may decide to stock up on food. The judgement informs the decision, and the judgement is always contextual.

We can adopt a more deliberate approach to seeing contexts by applying intuitive thinking. Intuitive thinking will pick up on our gut-feeling response to the environment and then consider it further. We may be at a dinner party and feel the occasion has become over-tense, and then seek to become a calming influence. We may recognise a degree of negativity in a family and decide to refrain from joining in any criticism. But to do this we must be able to pick up on the gut-feeling prompt and know how to respond to it.

In order to pick up on the context we must be able to consider not just what is obvious and apparent, but also what is unobvious or hidden from direct inspection. Logic allows us to say what is, but intuition allows us to consider what is missing. Many actions that seem right at the time may not seem so right when the context has changed. If everyone wants to go to war, or get into debt, or smoke cigarettes, or to invest in tulip bulbs, then anyone who opposes this form of behaviour will seem either foolish or ignorant. Logic cannot deal with contexts because it cannot see them, but intuition can.

Some of the worst periods of history, such as the pogroms, the witch hunts and the inquisitions, occurred because those who engaged in them were convinced that they were eradicating evil. They were convinced that they were on the side of truth and anyone who was against them was on the side of untruth and evil. The inability to see this comes from a very limited view of the world rather than from truth itself, arises because we cannot see the context which informs our judgements. The saying 'it seemed like a good idea at the time' is an expression of this.

One of the most difficult things in life is to maintain a sense of perspective, and maintaining a sense of perspective means being able to see beyond the current moment, the present trend, or the prevailing fashion. This form of 'seeing', is intuitive. Better intuition means making better judgements, about ourselves, others and society, and most of all about the actions we take in life.

The Inner Life

You are a policeman. Your wife's birthday is coming up, and you know she likes antique jewellery. You go to an antique shop and see a silver necklace with a ruby pendant in the shape of a pear. You decide she will like it and you buy it. Then on the course of your duties you visit a frail old woman who tells you she was burgled a year ago. She tells you she reported it at the time, but she didn't know that a silver necklace with a ruby pendant in the shape of a pear was also taken, and so she didn't report it. You take notes and you tell her you will look into it. That night you confide in your wife; you tell her it is probably the same necklace you bought for her birthday. Your wife says it's a pity, because she really likes the necklace. What would you do?

We cannot observe the inner life in the same way we can observe the outer world. We can observe a bird or a flower without affecting what we observe; a bird will not alter its behaviour because it is being watched. But our inner life is different; if we try to recall an action that we are ashamed of, such as when we were unkind to another person, we will find it uncomfortable, and may even find ourselves trying to ignore or dismiss the memory from our recollection.

Why would we want to observe our inner life? After all there is plenty in the outer world to demand our attention. From the moment we wake up, to going out to work, to coping with the demands of the day, to finding something to eat and then arriving home, the outer world makes constant demands on our attention, and perhaps more so than the inner life.

But life is about more than just food and a job and place to live; it is also about what we think and feel, and what we think and feel can determine whether a day is good or bad, whether we are hopeful or fearful about the future, or whether we regard our life as a failure or a success. As much as holding down a job and paying the bills is important, attending to the inner life is equally important, and perhaps more so, because its neglect has its consequences.

We can live well enough with little or no direct attention to either the outer world or the inner life. Much of life is routine; we can drive a car, read a newspaper, watch a television program or eat a meal, and we can do all of this automatically and with little attention. We can allow habit and routine to dictate not just our actions, but also our reactions to events and people. We can become angry if another person walks into a heated room on a cold day and leaves the door open; we can be highly offended by a careless remark, and we can be irritated by our neighbour's dog. All of this can happen with little or no attention to our inner life; indeed, it could be said that this form of reaction is the product of automatic and absent-minded behaviour.

While it is possible to live for days without really attending to what we do, there are times when we have to actively attend to life, both outwardly and inwardly. We might find ourselves driving in thick fog, or suddenly find ourselves in a violent environment, or realise a dispute with a neighbour has become all-consuming. It is then that we have to reflect and adjust our behaviour accordingly.

Just as there are times when we have to attend to the outer world, there are times when we have to attend to the inner life. We may find ourselves having to recall an event in order to report it to an authority. We may find ourselves having to consider the right choice of words for a eulogy at a funeral. We may find ourselves considering our emotions in order to prepare for an inevitable conflict with a friend or colleague. On occasions like this, we have to do more than simply allow thoughts and emotions to go unobserved and unattended; we have to reflect on them for a specific aim or purpose.

If our inner life consisted of only what we think, then logic would be enough to help us to observe and understand it. But our inner life includes not just what we think, but also our dreams, desires, fantasies, motives, instinctive reactions and emotional responses. And much of this is disorganised, contradictory and irrational. What is more, our irrational nature affects our choices and decisions as much, and perhaps more so, as reason and logic. It follows that if we are to attend to the inner life, then we need more than logic; we need intuition.

We do not just choose an item of clothing, look for a job or search for a partner, we do so with the image in mind of what our life will be like when we have made the choice and found the clothing, the job or the partner. Imagination informs our actions as much as necessity. To be able to observe our inner life fully, we have to be willing to see it as it is, wholly and fully, with all its contradictions and blemishes, and without attempting to apply logic where none exists.

This is essential not just for the more irrational elements of the inner life, but also for the hidden elements of the inner life. Because we have memories which hurt when we recall them, and motives we do not like to admit even to ourselves, there are elements of our inner life which we do not like to consider too closely. Logic cannot deal with these hidden elements, because logic cannot scrutinise what we cannot see openly and clearly. Only intuition, through progressive insight, can bring this hidden element out into the open. And we have to see it; we will see it sooner or later, because the more hidden elements play an important part in our decisions, judgements and actions. If we act out of revenge, we may deny it, but it is still revenge, and revenge has its consequences.

We can sometimes see this hidden element when we look back on our past actions through hindsight. Hindsight reflection will sometimes reveal that we were motivated by thoughts and emotions we would not admit to ourselves at the time. We may have been motivated by the desire for jealousy or hatred, however much we might have told ourselves we were acting out of nobler motives. Emotions such as jealousy or hatred often only become apparent in hindsight, when the strength of the emotion has waned and we are able to see the situation more objectively. This can be painful, and it is only by seeing our motives clearly that we can avoid the worst excesses of our behaviour.

This hidden element of our inner life is not caused by a lack of logic, but is actually caused by the very nature of logic itself. The certainty of logic comes from dividing the world into right and wrong, and the more certain we are of being right, the less chance we will have of seeing any error in our own actions. If we regard ourselves as good then we cannot see ourselves as bad, and consequently we will not allow ourselves to see anything in our inner life which contradicts our image of ourselves as a good person. While logic prevents us from accepting contradictions, intuition is more inclusive, and it allows us to see both the good and bad elements simply by attending to what is there.

Gut-feeling will prompt us when there is something about our inner life which is presently hidden from us.

If we try to understand what gut-feeling is telling us, we may be prompted to look further to try to discover what the hidden element might be. Then further intuitive thinking can bring this hidden element out into the open through insight, and we suddenly see what we previously couldn't see or perhaps didn't want to see.

You are a rambler and you enjoy walking through the countryside. One of the landowners does not like you crossing their land, so they put up a 'private' notice on the wooden gate leading to their property. You know you are entitled to walk along a footpath which has been created over centuries, and so you are not put off by this; you open the gate, enter and then close it behind you. Then the landowner puts a lock on the gate, but this still does not deter you. Then the landowner makes the gate higher, and they put barbed wire up along either side of the fence to stop you climbing over, so you climb over the high gate instead. Then the landowner takes down the barbed wire, unlocks the gate, removes the 'private' notice, and replaces it with a sign that reads 'Enter at your own risk'. Would you enter?

If we cannot see our inner life clearly, this hidden element governs our actions in a way which we are not fully aware of. This hidden element is often the less rational side to our nature, such as our fears, suspicions, desires and fantasies. The inability to see, clearly and fully, this less rational side to our inner life has its consequences, one of which is that we can be manipulated by it.

In addition to our emotional responses, there are elements of our inner life we do not like to look at too closely. We do not like to see our own failings, errors and stupidities. And yet we can see the same failings in others without difficulty. What is more, we can observe not just another person's failings, but we can observe how they too do not like to admit their failings, even to themselves. This blindness comes from logic, which divides the world into good and evil, right and wrong; if we can see another person's foolishness without difficulty, it is because we regard ourselves as intelligent.

This blindness is not merely theoretical, but very real, which is why it can be used against us. It is the basis of most of the manipulative practices we come across in life, including deception, manipulation, entrapment and emotional blackmail. If we cannot see that we have weaknesses, follies, unreal hopes and desires, then we can be certain others can.

The confidence trickster, or 'conman', will seek to gain our trust; once we trust them, we find it difficult to be suspicious of them. In the same way, the flatterer will seek to discover our insecurities and vanities, and then use them against us. And the demagogue will seek to exploit our fears and prejudices. The way to control people, both individuals and the masses, is to affect them unconsciously, without them suspecting the deception is taking place.

Manipulation is best achieved by appealing to the emotions directly. Emotions such as anger, fear or suspicion create a context through which all that follows will be seen in that light. If we suspect someone is a traitor, then everything they do and say will seem treacherous. If we regard someone as an enemy then everything they do will look like an act of aggression. If we adore someone, even their temper tantrums will seem adorable. The emotions colour what we think, and what we think affects how we interpret what we see.

Within limits, the need to control and govern the responses of other people is a natural part of life. It is the basis of civility and polite behaviour; if we want someone to do something for us and say 'please', it is more likely they will comply. If someone mocks us, we will let them know in no uncertain terms they have angered us, even if only to make the point that they should not do it again. Equally, the control and governance of others can also become unnatural, such as the manipulative practices of the confidence trickster, the extortionist and the flatterer. As with all things, it is a matter of personal judgement to decide if the control is reasonable or excessive. And that judgement is intuitive.

Intuition is much slower and less precise than logic. This makes for less certainty, but it makes for a more inclusive outlook. The intuitive mind can pick up on fear, and not feel the need to dismiss it, even if it is not based on anything real. If it is there, it must be taken into account, even if it proves to be unjustified. From the point of view of logic, admitting that fear is unfounded and at the same time real is a contradiction, but from the point of view of intuition, it is simply material for observation.

Intuitive judgement is fluid, conditional and inclusive, rather than single, fixed and defined. Intuitively we can accept that we can be considerate about others and yet still be selfish, or speak well of others and yet still harbour private criticisms of them. Intuitive thinking can admit to contradictions in our inner life because the contradictions are there. Logic wants us to decide one way or another.

The less obvious elements of our inner life are not unlike the enigmas of the outer world; they do not just jump out and announce themselves to us. We can be so certain that we already see and know everything that we will not stop to consider there might be anything we do not know or see. It is the same with our own opinion of ourselves. We can be quite certain that we know ourselves well, and do not feel the need to consider anything which is enigmatic, puzzling or contradictory about our own inner life. As with the enigmas of the outer world, we have to be willing to admit that this hidden element exists for us to be willing to begin to look for it.

Our first impression of an enigma, whether inner or outer, usually comes through gut-feeling, or the dim realisation that there is something that we do not see rightly or fully. With respect to the inner life, this can take the form of second thoughts about our motives for an action. Our motives are often mixed, and what we admit to ourselves is often only the more obvious aspects of a much more complex reality. While logic focuses on the more obvious aspects, intuition will pick up on what is less obvious, such as a brooding resentment, a hidden criticism or an underlying anger. That is why, in order to see such hidden elements, we have to prevent the logical mind from dominating our thinking. The secondary elements do not present themselves as forcefully as the more obvious elements, and yet the secondary elements can be just as influential in our judgements and actions as the reasons we give to ourselves for taking them.

If we do not attend to these secondary elements of our inner life, they can go unchecked until they become so obvious that even we cannot ignore them. It is from this that depression, addiction or negativity can become the defining feature in a person's character. It is interesting to note that others can often see this long before we can. What makes us most foolish is not that we see too little, but that we do not admit it. Intuitive reflection will allow us to consider what is not obvious and apparent, and if we are willing to engage in this when our gut-feeling prompts us to, we may at least save ourselves from acting foolishly. This is why self-knowledge is both intuitive and progressive; we find it difficult to observe our own inner life because seeing our own foolishness is not always funny.

Moods and Emotions

You grow up in a small town. On the street where you live is a beautiful girl. You see her daily and you get to know her name. You are secretly in love with her but you are too shy to tell her what you feel about her. Then one day she tells you she is leaving to go to university. You feel hurt because she is leaving, but you say nothing and you wish her well. Then the following summer you see her again and she tells you she is in a relationship. Again, you feel hurt but you say nothing and you wish her well. Then you discover she is going to be married. Now you feel really hurt and you wish you had been brave enough to tell her what you really felt about her. And then one day a friend tells you her fiancé has been killed in a car crash. Now how do you feel?

We are not normally aware of our emotions. We focus on the stuff of everyday life - what time it is, what we are going to eat, whether we are cold or warm and so on - and we give little attention to our moods and emotions. But they are always there, always acting as a kind of backdrop to all that we say and do. It is only when our emotions are pronounced or extreme that we pay direct attention to them. For the most part, extreme emotions are occasional or rare, and so we go about our day to day business and ignore our emotional life.

Moods and emotions are the context through which we act and speak and think. A mood is like the constant sound of traffic or the light in a room; it provides the context for the specific actions that take place within it. If we live in a rowdy neighbourhood, our actions will reflect that. If the pavement is busy, we will feel the need to walk quickly rather than to stop and browse at leisure. The context determines the action, and it does this largely through our emotional response to it. If the sun is out, we might decide to go for a walk, and then if we look out and check the sky and see rain clouds, we might change our mind.

A mood will determine whether we regard a statement as irritating or amusing, or whether a bus ride is boring or relaxing, or whether a hard day at work is frustrating or a good day done. A good mood will determine whether we regard a shelter in the rain as a blessing, a bad-tempered neighbour as a reminder of our own good fortune, or an illness as a reminder to get well and enjoy life again. Moods and emotions are not specific like tables and chairs, but like music or the seasons, always fluid and changing, and for that reason logic deals badly with them.

Most of our emotions are low-key. We may be aware of a degree of stress when we are about to do something new, such as driving a car for the first time, but unless it is excessive, we will be unable to get a fix on it. Low-key emotions are difficult to define, and for that reason they affect our actions unconsciously. In addition to being difficult to pin down, our emotions are not constant in the way the physical world is constant. We can go from being mildly irritated in one minute to being outright angry the next, or from being mildly curious about a person's motives to being highly suspicious about them moments later. Because we are trained to think in terms of fixed definitions and certainties, we find it difficult to relate to our emotions when they do not operate in this manner.

Socially, the expression of emotions is seen as a burden. Emotions interfere with level-headed decision making, planning, good manners and dignified behaviour. We try to limit the expression of emotions in public, at least to those which are deemed socially acceptable. We may express emotion at a leaving party, or at a funeral or a football match, but not at a business meeting or a bus queue. Indeed, any outward expression of emotion which is out of keeping with the context is regarded as an indication that an individual is not wholly rational or sensible.

This attitude towards the emotional life is, in part, due to the dominance of logic in society. We regard a logical mind as a sign of intellectual superiority, and those who govern society, from the academic, to the judge, to the government official, are all portrayed as logical and rational beings who keep their subjective emotions in check. It is for this reason that we claim to make decisions and judgements based on sound reason and logic rather than emotional feeling. Many discussions, arguments and witness statements are made as though there is no emotional element involved, and yet of course they are. From a logical perspective, the emotions are like an unwanted guest at a party.

The inability to deal with our emotions results in a one-sided view of what we are as human beings. It affects not just how we see ourselves, but how we deal with others, and indeed how we think about the society we live in. If we assume that reason should dictate society, we will be surprised when our assumptions do not turn out as expected. We rarely calculate resentment, anger or dissent in our political manifestos, and we rarely take the inner life into account when we create factories, towns and cities. And yet the emotions inform everything we do, and we understand very little about human nature unless we take the emotional life into account. When we claim to be rational and law-abiding, we overlook the fact that hope and fear are as real as laws and prisons.

The emotions affect not simply our direct experience of life, but our plans and ambitions and attitude towards life. We do not just read and learn, we do so in the belief that we might gain something from the venture. Our political, religious or scientific views are based as much on how they resonate with us emotionally as on their rational or logical content. If we cannot see the influence of the emotions on life, it is not because they are absent, but because we are blind to them. And we are blind to them because we are trained to think logically, and logic is insufficient to deal with the emotions.

Logic will tell us that we should flag down a taxi in the rain, but it will not tell us it is because we don't like rain. Logic will tell us to sort out our finances, but it will not tell us that we are doing so out of anxiety. Logic will tell us to criticise a statement, but it will not tell us it is because the statement irritates us. If we want to understand the emotions, logic doesn't help. In order to deal with the emotions, we have to employ intuitive thinking.

You discover your partner's diary; you didn't know they had a diary. Your partner is out, and now you can read it and know their innermost thoughts. You have had good times and bad times with your partner, and there was even a time when you suspected they were cheating on you. Now you have their diary in your hands and you can know for certain whether they were or not. If you discover that your suspicions were correct, you will not be able to hide it, and it will be the end of your relationship. Even if you read it and discover nothing, and your partner asks you if you have ever read their diary, you would have to explain why you read it, or lie to them. Would you read it or not?

When we find ourselves in a situation which is complex or confusing, logic demands that we put our emotions to one side and make any decisions on a purely rational basis. The problem with this approach is that even if our logic is good, we will still feel the complexity of the situation through our emotions. We feel this because our emotions are no less real than our thoughts. While logic dismisses the emotions as either irrelevant or misleading, the intuitive mind accepts them as one element in a greater whole. When this occurs, we refer to it as the head telling us one thing and the heart telling us another.

Our emotional life is complex because life itself is complex. We can sit in a sunny garden and feel stressed, and we can sit in a prison cell and feel content. The quality of life is not defined by the outer world alone, but by our inner response to it. How we respond to a situation depends on how we see it. We can hear an unkind remark and feel offended by it or we can dismiss it as unimportant. What is more, the same remark can offend us one day and amuse us the next. Life isn't simple because our inner life isn't simple. In order to deal with the complexity of our inner life, we have to accept it for what it is; anything less will limit our understanding of ourselves and, more particularly, our motives for making the decision.

Our moods are complex because they are affected not just by how we feel but also by the moods of others around us. We will feel different in an office, a church, or a football stadium. We may detect cynicism in another person and respond in kind, or we may detect a degree of nervousness in them and act sympathetically. Our own emotions can be as much affected by what others feel as by what we feel directly.

In addition to the moods of others, there is the wider mood of times we live in, which is sometimes called the 'zeitgeist'. Conflict and recession, prosperity and good times, all of this can affect the mood of both individuals and groups, and it can do this in both a positive or negative sense. The more optimistic elements tend to find expression through music and the arts. The two World Wars and the Great Depression of the twentieth century were accompanied by a noted optimism in the music and films of the period. The more negative elements tend to find expression through politics and the media. Both elements can coexist in society and both can inform the attitudes and opinions prevalent at the time.

We pick up on background emotions through gut-feeling. If we want to understand the emotions however, we have to apply intuitive insight. Insight is much slower than logic – we have to remain open to new thoughts and ideas to see what is presently hidden – and by its very nature it is more suited to helping us to understand the emotional life. If we are in the middle of an argument, we may be consumed by a more immediate emotion such as anger or hurt or betrayal. It is only later, when the more dominant emotions have receded, that we are able to put the emotional element into perspective.

The emotions can be studied just as the weather or social behaviour can be studied. If we take an interest in a subject – any subject, whether it is music or gardening - our understanding will develop over time. Our first attempts to understand the emotions – however clumsy – will, if pursued intuitively, eventually lead to a better grasp of the details and a fuller view of the whole. It is similar in approach to studying a foreign language; at first, we pick up on a few words and phrases, and then if we are persistent, we will expand our knowledge to include nuances, appropriate phrases and interesting terms. The more obvious emotions – irritation, anger and fear – are easiest to become aware of, while less obvious emotions – subtle boredom, resentfulness and apathy – require a degree of familiarity and self-knowledge.

Studying and understanding the emotions does not mean we will become irrational or subjective, but simply that we will be better informed about what is going on in our own inner life. We can deal best with the emotions by seeing them clearly, not by denying they exist.

If we are out of touch with our emotions, or if we feel emotionally dead it is because we are not listening to the intuitive mind. We can hear a wonderful piece of music, stand in front of a great work of art or even listen to a person speak passionately about a subject which is of concern to them and yet not be moved by it. For the same reason we can eat a meal without tasting it, we can also live on autopilot emotionally, at least until they finally surface in a violent or forceful way. To be in touch with our emotions, we have to be aware of them; intuition is the means to get in touch with our emotions.

If we are not aware of our emotions, we can be guided by them and assume we are acting and thinking rationally. It is interesting to observe that most arguments, whether personal, political or theoretical are emotionally motivated, and yet those who engage in such arguments are rarely willing to admit this. As much as we pride ourselves on our reason and logic, we are very much creatures of emotion.

Conscience

You are walking through the countryside and you see a barn on fire. The local fire department is in town, but it is many miles away and there is no one else around. You hear a dog barking inside the barn. You rush up to the barn and you see flames and thick black smoke inside. You can't see the dog but you can hear it bark. You put your head down and head for the sound of the dog. On your way, you see a holdall on the floor. The holdall is open and there are bundles of banknotes inside. You realise there must be a fortune inside the holdall. You grab the holdall, but it is heavy and it takes both hands to lift. The fire is spreading and you can no longer hear the sound of the dog. Do you take the holdall and get out or do you continue towards the dog?

We use the word 'conscience' to refer to situations when we feel uneasy about a decision, a judgement or a course of action. If the decision or choice is simple, such as whether we should defend ourselves from an attacker, then there will be little to trouble our conscience. But if the decision is a complex one, such as whether we should report a close friend to the police, then we may be highly troubled by our conscience. To be troubled by our conscience means that we think not just about the action, but about our motives for taking the action.

The word 'conscience' means 'with knowledge'. The knowledge which conscience refers to is knowledge of the inner life, or rather to act with full knowledge of our motives and intentions. If we are not aware of our motives for taking an action, or if we deceive ourselves about our motives, then we may act without a conscience. So, to act with a conscience means firstly to be able to see our motives clearly, and secondly to be honest with ourselves about what we are seeing.

It might seem strange to suggest that we can act with anything less than with full knowledge of our motives. After all, there are no walls or doors to prevent us from seeing our motives directly. If we are unkind to others, there is no third party hiding our unkindness from us. Yet we do not always see our motives clearly, and if we do, we often see them partially and incompletely. The phenomenon of hindsight, when we look back on our actions long after the event, can sometimes reveal an underlying motive of which we were vaguely aware at the time but would not admit to ourselves. When this happens, it can be highly instructive, and it can tell us something about how our view of ourselves can be very limited and selective.

Just as we can be deceived by others, we can also deceive ourselves. The method employed by the stage magician, known as 'misdirection', where the attention of the audience is directed away from an area of interest, can also apply to the inner life. We do not like to look at any element of our inner life which is unpleasant. Our natural optimism means that we prefer to see ourselves in a better light, and anything which contradicts that view is either overlooked or ignored. Conscience therefore, requires us to see both the good and bad in ourselves, and of course this is not always pleasant.

The division into what pleases or displeases us is in part natural; we seek what is pleasant and beneficial, and recoil at anything unpleasant or unhealthy. But this division into pleasant and unpleasant can be greatly enhanced by logic. Logic divides what we see into 'is' and 'is not', and it causes us to reject anything that we do not like as 'wrong'. So, we can have all the information at our disposal, and if we focus only on what pleases us, we will ignore or even reject what displeases us.

Just as many situations in life are highly complex, our inner life is also highly complex. We can have very mixed motives. We can admire someone for their beauty, or for their personality, or sometimes for a mixture of both reasons. We can care about someone and yet have selfish motives for doing so. We can speak well of someone in order to hide our critical views of them, or criticise someone because we care about them. The complexity of our inner life is not helped by the polarising nature of logic. That is why, if we want to see our motives clearly, we have to employ intuition.

Applying intuition means we can accept that our motives might be mixed, confused or even contradictory and not feel the need to sort them into good or bad. We can feel both anger and concern when we are hurt by someone we like; we can regard a confrontation as unnecessary and yet inevitable, and we can admit that love can be both affectionate and sexual. If we think intuitively, it will allow us to see our inner life, and particularly our motives, more completely.

It follows that intuition is essential if we want to act in light of conscience, or 'with knowledge'. Just as deception in the outer world means that we see too little, deception in the inner life, or self-deception, means that we see too little and do not stop to consider what we might be overlooking or ignoring. It is when this hidden element becomes obvious, and in a moment of hindsight we suddenly see what previously we would not admit to ourselves at the time, that we have the experience that we call 'being troubled by our conscience'. Conscience is seeing, and seeing means looking intuitively at our inner life.

You are in a time of war; enemy forces are about to enter the city. There is a ship waiting at the harbour but you do not have a boarding pass. You go to a nearby pub where you see an old man sitting alone

142

and you go across and join him. He is wearing an expensive overcoat and he has a heavy gold watch. There is a large glass of whiskey in front of him and he is already quite drunk. He tells you he once had a mansion and a yacht and now all he has is his coat, his watch and his boarding pass. He curses aloud and then swallows the last of the whiskey, and then passes out. The ship sounds its horn to announce it is about to leave. You shake the old man but he does not respond. You see the boarding pass in his pocket.
Would you take it?

We use the words 'conscience' and 'morality' in the same sense and often in the same sentence. It would be easy to assume they are the same, but there is a very important difference between them. Morality is about how we relate to the outer world and conscience is about how we relate to our inner life.

Society is governed by morality rather than conscience. This is because morality is cultural but conscience is personal. Morality is concerned with right and wrong behaviour, and right and wrong are determined by society rather than by the individual. For society to determine what is right or wrong for everyone, there has to be consistency and uniformity. Without consistency and uniformity, individuals would have to decide whether an action was right or wrong depending on how they felt about it, so from the point of view of morality, what is wrong for one person must be wrong for another, quite apart from how they feel about the action or circumstance.

The dominance of morality as the means to determine whether an action is right or wrong comes from religion. The modern era is largely secular or non-religious, but most of what we regard as moral comes from religious culture. It is still wrong to kill or steal or bear false witness, but owing to the secularisation of society we can now buy and sell goods on the Sabbath. Religion adopted this approach because individuals, left to their own devices, were regarded as prone to sinning, and so they had to be guided by a higher authority in order for them to know what was right or wrong. Even now, in secular society, the dominant approach is to guide individual behaviour by morality rather than by personal conscience.

One of the problems with this approach is that morality can only deal with behaviour in black and white terms, so if an action is deemed 'good' then it cannot be questioned. This creates a highly polarised view of right and wrong, where good is always good and bad is always bad. When the world was relatively unchanging, or when change occurred over centuries, it was possible to define right and wrong in absolute terms. But the world is changing, and at a rate unknown to previous generations. Slavery was acceptable in European culture up until the nineteenth century; now it is morally reprehensible. In the nineteenth century it was morally right to smack a child and in the twentieth century it was regarded as a form of child-abuse. In the nineteenth century it was moral to condemn homosexuality and in the twentieth century it was immoral to condemn homosexuality.

Logic cannot cope with changing circumstances because logic cannot accept that something may be right in one circumstance and wrong in another. But intuition can do this. This is why morality is logical and conscience is intuitive.

Intuition is the watching mind, and the more active our intuitive mind, the more we will see the complexity of our inner life. We may not commit adultery because we believe it is wrong, or we may not commit adultery because we are afraid of being caught. We may pay someone a compliment because we think well of them or we may pay them a compliment in order to flatter them. The outward action may be the same, but only our conscience will tell us what the motive for the action is. We can judge a person's morality, but not their conscience; that is for them to decide. A person can remain silent when they witness an injustice, and yet still give the appearance of being an honest person. We see only the action and do not see what is hidden in the inner life, so of course we cannot judge another person's conscience.

If we are governed by our conscience, whether we regard an action as right or wrong will depend not on how it is regarded socially, but on how we feel about it. This is not an excuse for moral relativism, but merely a statement about how conscience works. Conscience means to act 'with knowledge' and to act with knowledge means to see our inner life in all its complexity. The reason why our more important and difficult decisions in life are intuitive is because many of them involve matters of conscience.

If our conscience will not allow us to fight in a war, others may die because of this. If we know a person has become suicidal, we may take a knife from them without their approval. What determines whether an action is moral or immoral is how it is seen by others, but what determines whether an action is born out of conscience is determined by how we see it. If morality is simple black and white, conscience is complex, conditional and dependent on how much we feel emotionally about the circumstance or action.

If we act immorally, we have to live with the consequence of being caught. But if we act against our conscience, we have to live with the consequences even if no one else witnesses the act.

Acting against our conscience has a further consequence; if we act against our conscience, we will be ashamed of our actions, and this will limit our ability to see ourselves clearly. The development of intuition and an honest conscience go hand in hand. The feeling of guilt is often our conscience prompting us to see what we would prefer to ignore. To act with a conscience is to have a healthy intuition.

It can happen that a person can act out of conscience but is regarded as immoral by society. Galileo Galilei (1564 - 1642), for example, was tried and charged with heresy by the Inquisition; he is now regarded as the one of the founders of modern science. Nelson Mandela (1918 - 2013) was arrested and sentenced to life imprisonment for conspiring to overthrow the state. He later became President of South Africa. The degree to which we are guided by morality or by conscience is a personal one. Our conscience may put us at odds with society, or at least with the governing authority. Some of the worst periods of history, from the witch hunts to the pogroms, to the inquisitions have been marked by the moral righteousness of those conducting the persecutions. Absolute right and wrong are the product of morality. Conscience, like intuition, is very personal.

To have a conscience does not mean we will be good people or even that we will always act rightly; it just means that we see our inner life more clearly. Having a healthy intuition will not make us free of the darker elements of human nature any more than having good eyesight will remove the obstacles in a road.

If people-watching is the intuitive mind observing others, conscience is the intuitive mind observing the self. The question is not what we see, but what we do not see. The intuitive mind reveals these hidden aspects of our inner life in the way it reveals the hidden aspects of an enigma or of the inner life of others. We have to remain sufficiently fluid in our thinking and open to new ideas for the insights to arrive.

The hidden elements of our inner life are hidden because we attend to what pleases us, and turn from what displeases us. The more confident we are that we understand ourselves well, and particularly that we are good and moral people, the less we will be able to see any time or occasion when we were being less than honourable. This can be painful, and yet failure can be a blessing, particularly if we learn from it.

Intuitive thinking is progressive and insightful. If we apply intuitive thinking, we may see today what we could not see yesterday. If we are not willing to see our inner life clearly, we may act today in a way that we come to regret tomorrow. Conscience does not make us better people, just better-informed people.

Insight

You are a pilot in a war. Your plane has been shot down and you are alone on a small island. Your plane went down in the sea, along with all your equipment, and now you have no means to communicate with the outside world. There are enough trees on the island to find shelter but not enough to provide sustenance. You have enough fresh water to last for a few days. From time to time you see a plane flying overhead but you don't have binoculars and so you don't know whether it is an enemy plane or not. You could make an 'SOS' sign out of branches, but if it is an enemy plane, they might see it and try to kill you. What would you do?

The assumption of logic is that in order to solve a problem, all we have to do is examine the evidence, scrutinise it, weed out any errors, weigh up the alternatives and then decide. The problem with this approach is that we do not always have all the available information. Logic can deal with what we know, but we cannot examine or scrutinise what we do not know.

We can solve many problems logically. If we are in financial difficulty then we can examine our finances, cut down on any luxury items, find cheaper sources, be careful about unnecessary spending and then find ways to increase our income. All of this is logical. Provided we have enough information, provided our thinking is sound, and provided the existing solutions work, and then logic will solve the problem for us.

This is the method taught at school and it is the basis of the examination system; we read the question carefully, examine the information provided, weed out any errors, weigh up the alternatives and then provide the right answer. But life is not like school. In life, we rarely have all the information needed to make a decision. When we do not have enough information, or when the information we have is inadequate, or when we are faced with a new situation, or when the existing solutions do not work, we have to try a different approach.

Insight operates very differently from logic. A logical solution comes from considering what we already know, whereas an insight solution comes from considering what we do not know. The hallmark of an insight solution is that it often arrives instantly and without warning. A flash of insight will suddenly reveal what we did not see and could not have imagined beforehand. This is because insight does not come from examining what we know, but from seeing what is presently hidden from us. It is rather like the misdirection of the stage magician; insight allows us to see what is being overlooked by our present focus. This is why an insight solution will provide a wholly new and unexpected perspective on a problem.

For those trained to think logically, insight is difficult to understand. The idea that a solution can arrive out of nowhere, without any reasoning or logical justification, is contrary to the very basis of logic. Owing to the dominance of logic in mainstream education, the importance of insight is either overlooked, ignored or misunderstood. And when it is too obvious to dismiss, it is usually regarded as a kind of fluke or the product of wayward genius. And yet insight has played a part in some of the most important developments in the history of thought.

Insight was responsible for Archimedes running naked from his bath, shouting 'Eureka!'. It was responsible for the theorem of Pythagoras, who is said to have sacrificed oxen for the epiphany. Insight was also responsible for Newton's concept of gravity, triggered by his observation of a falling apple. It was responsible for Rowan Hamilton's quaternions; the idea occurred to him so instantly that he carved the equation into a nearby stone in case he forgot it. It was responsible for Goethe's theory of colour; an idea that occurred to him so powerfully that he announced instantly that Newton's theory was false. And it was responsible for Tesla's alternating current motor; the image of which appeared so boldly to him that he was able to imagine it running forwards and backwards. Each explanation, idea or theory arrived whole and without precedent, and each caused the existing explanation, idea or theory to be wholly superseded or abandoned immediately on its arrival.

Insight was also responsible for many of the inventions of the Industrial revolution; many of the inventors of the period were untrained amateurs, and often working in a different field from their given invention. The steam engine was invented by Thomas Newcomen (1664 - 1729), an ironmonger; the seed drill was invented by Jethro Tull (1674 - 1741), a farmer; the marine chronometer was invented by John Harrison (1693 - 1776), a carpenter; the flying shuttle was invented by John Kay (1704 - 1779), a reed maker; the spinning jenny was invented by James Hargreaves (1720 - 1778), another carpenter; the spinning frame came from Richard Arkwright (1732 - 1792), a barber; Samuel Crompton (1753 - 1827), who gave us the spinning mule was a musician, and the cotton gin was invented by Eli Whitney (1765 - 1825), a teacher.

Invention doesn't come from academic analysis and the defence of existing methods and practices, but from questioning and challenging the limitations of what is presently known and from looking for new methods and alternatives. Insight is the gift of those who question the existing explanations, ideas and methods, not those who defend them.

And yet in spite of this, insight is barely acknowledged and barely touched on in present day education. This is because academics are trained to explain and defend the existing ideas and outlooks, and it is the nature of insight to question and challenge them. An insight can instantly make the older point of view look outdated and redundant. It is not surprising that mainstream education finds insight difficult to understand, not least because the new perspectives it offers threaten the existing order.

Insight is not limited to gifted individuals and geniuses; it can occur to any individual, of any station, education or standing. It is not confined to inventions, theories and discoveries, but to any problem which requires new thinking. We may be troubled by lesser matters such as the behaviour of another, the cause of an illness, an emergent trend in society, or a personal moral dilemma. If we find the existing explanations or solutions to be inadequate, we may decide to consider new approaches and new ideas. This means being able to question what we know and what we assume to be right. It means looking again at what we know or thought we understood. If we consider what we do not know rather than what we do know, we may find ourselves fortunate to be in receipt of insight.

You are walking alone through the mountains and you come across a ravine. The ravine is three metres wide and very deep. You look across the ravine and decide it is too wide to risk jumping across. There are plenty of rocks and shrubs on your side but very little on the other side of the ravine other than grass and dirt. You have a heavy rucksack with you, a knife and nine metres of rope. You have been walking for a week and you are nearly out of food. You doubt you would be able to survive the return journey. What would you do?

If we want to think about a problem for which there is no obvious or existing solution, we have to use our imagination. The creative use of the imagination is quite different from the application of logic, not least because we cannot come up with new ideas by examining the existing methods. To think creatively we have to consider what doesn't exist, and from a logical point of view this is wrong.

New ideas often come only after we have examined the existing methods and possibilities and found them wanting. We may try to modify the existing methods and solutions, remove anything that doesn't work, and then try out the new or modified method, but if this proves unsatisfactory then we have to think creatively. When we do, we have to move beyond the limitations of what is known and consider what is unknown or what might be possible. And that means we have to weaken the hold of logic on our thinking; that is why early criticism can kill a creative idea.

In order to use imagination to solve a problem, it has to be deliberate and directed. It cannot be of the passive, daydreaming type of imagination, simply because passive daydreaming will soon wander off the point and we will lose our focus. We have to attend to our imaginative thinking just as we have to attend to our logical or mathematical thinking. This means we have to employ the intuitive mind to direct our imagination to the problem at hand. The relationship between intuition and imagination is the reason why intuition is associated with invention, inspiration, creative ideas and insight.

Searching for a new idea is not unlike looking for enigmas. When we first see an enigma, we see little more than a possibility. Something about the enigma tells us there is more to what we see than meets the eye, but we cannot say what the hidden element is. Nonetheless an enigma hints at the possibility of new knowledge, and that is why it can capture our imagination. It is important to keep the logical mind in check; if we apply criticism, particularly at the early stages, we will simply limit what we see to what we already know. The enigma prompts us to think about what we presently do not know or see, and so we have to be open to the possibilities provided by it.

As with enigmas, new ideas do not just jump out and announce themselves to us. We have to actively look for new ideas. What is more, we have to make a habit of looking for new ideas; passive observation of the world will not reveal what is hidden or unnoticed. Many inventors had more than one patent to their name; Nikola Tesla (1856 - 1943) had over three hundred patents, and Thomas Edison (1847 - 1931) had more than a thousand. Actively looking for new ideas is like actively observing other people or actively attending to what we see when walking along a high street.

In addition to looking for new ideas, we have to nurture them by considering them before passing judgement on them. New ideas can seem ephemeral and weak when they first occur to us. What is more, they can seem, initially, less satisfactory than existing ideas, particularly when we are very familiar with the existing ideas and know what their outcomes and applications are. In the initial stages of looking for new ideas, we have to entertain thoughts which are not as solid or certain as existing ideas. This is why looking for new ideas can often seem like looking for a shadowy figure in a darkened room. In some respects, this is exactly what we are doing. Creative imagination means directing our attention to what we do not yet know or cannot yet see clearly.

Insight occurs when the full potential of the new idea suddenly presents itself to us. The potential was always there; the first inklings of the new idea might have caught our attention, but the ability to see the full value of it will depend on our perspective, or on how much we value the new idea. Insight occurs when our perspective suddenly changes, and instantly we see what was initially ephemeral from a new and very different point of view. This is why insight is sometimes described as a blinding flash of light, an inspiration, or an epiphany. What has changed is not the idea itself, but our perception of it. This sudden change in perception is what is sometimes called a 'eureka moment'.

This sudden change in perception can be both shocking and emotional. We are not normally aware of the emotions that accompany our attitudes and assumptions because they form part of the background to our thinking and judgement. This is why many arguments are highly emotional; each side will adopt not just a point of view, but all the emotional content that goes with it. If we become free of a perspective, we also become free of the accompanying emotion. This is why the new outlook provided by insight can be accompanied by a feeling of liberation and even euphoria. This emotional element is what caused Archimedes to run naked from his bath, why Goethe spoke aloud, and why the physicist Fritjof Capra burst into laughter on receipt of his insight. The effect is not unlike the laughter at hearing the punchline to a joke; we hear the punchline and, seeing what was previously hidden from us, burst out laughing.

Intuitively we know that there is much we cannot see directly. For the most part this feeling remains unconscious and unattended as we go about the business of day to day life. It is only when we are forced to consider the hidden or unseen element directly, when our existing methods and solutions do not work, or when our present understanding proves inadequate, that we begin to think about what we do not know or cannot see. Galileo was not the first to observe a swinging chandelier, but he was the first to openly question why it did so.

The phenomenon of insight is perhaps the clearest indication that we do not see the world in its entirety. If we saw the world in its entirety, insight would not be possible. The phenomenon of insight tells us that the limitations are not in the outer world, but in our thinking, or in the way we see the world. Logic deals with the world we know, but intuition deals with the world we don't know. A powerful insight can provide not just a solution to a problem, but a new means to see and understand the world

Outcomes

You are in prison and you are due to be executed in the morning. You have been given your last meal, and you are now waiting alone in your cell. The prison warden comes along and hands you a pen and paper. They tell you that you can write a last letter, and you can write anything you want. Your first thoughts are that this is a pointless exercise; you are going to die in the morning and so it doesn't matter what you write. But you are alone in your cell, and this is your last night alive and you are unable to sleep. You keep looking at the paper and pen. You have the opportunity to sum up your whole life in a single letter. What would you write?

Many people take the view that it doesn't matter what we think; what matters is what we do or what we achieve in life. From this point of view, what we think is merely personal and part of our inner life, and not as important as holding down a day job, paying the bills, owning a home and then finding enough time for pleasure or entertainment. But what we think matters at least as much as what we do, and in many respects even more so.

There are many things that thinking will not change. It will not change the weather or free us from the need to earn a living, and it will not take away the inevitability of death. None of this will change because of what we think, and yet what we think can greatly affect how we respond to the conditions we find ourselves in, and whether we regard an experience as a necessity or an enjoyment. We can look back over our life much as we might look back on a meal we have just finished, and realise we have eaten it and yet tasted very little of it. A deathbed is not the best place to think about how we intend to live, and so what we think matters a great deal.

Perhaps more important than what we think is how we think. If what we think amounts to little more than having political or religious views and opinions, then we may find ourselves on our deathbed with very little more than just a collection of opinions. The thinking that allows us to attend to the moment, to savour the taste, and to experience life to the full, is intuitive thinking.

Intuition is the watching mind. In order to attend fully, both to the outer world and the inner life, we have to engage the intuitive mind. To live with attention means to be active intuitively. A meal can be just a meal, and a walk along a street can be no more than just a walk along the street if the intuitive mind is passive. We can sleepwalk through life, or we can live it with active attention; the outcome will still be the deathbed, but the difference will be between a life wasted and a life enjoyed.

Intuitive thinking is what makes us most human. It allows us to reflect not just on the outer world, but also on our inner life. This inner reflection, provided it is done with attention, is by no means morbid or a waste of time. We can only alter our behaviour by reflecting on what we have done, and in that way shape what we would like to do, and then decide what we need to do to change it. If we could not reflect in this way, we would be no more than machines.

Any activity has an outcome. If we invest time in gardening or in painting, we will develop both technique and understanding, and then be able to employ this to our advantage. In the same way, if we invest time in our intuitive thinking, we will come to develop a greater understanding of what intuition is and how to employ it in daily life. Reading a book like this can help, but as with gardening or painting, it is the application of intuition that makes the most difference both to our ability and to our understanding of the subject.

It has been necessary to point to the dominance of logic again and again throughout this book. This is because we are born into a world where logic is regarded as the highest form of thinking and anything which does not pass the test of logic is regarded as either immature, subjective or emotional. We have been trained to think in this way from a very young age, and indeed it is the very basis of the school curriculum. This means that anyone who arrives at a position of authority in society will not only have developed the ability to think logically, but they will have accepted the values and methods associated with logic. It is for this reason that logic informs law, economics, politics, religion, science and philosophy.

As individuals, the dominance of logic means that we think logically as a matter of course. We assume that if we want to think clearly, we have to think logically. It also means we assume that the purpose of thinking is to arrive at the right answer, rather than a balanced view. And it means that we see the world in terms of right and wrong. If we accept all of this without question then we will inevitably assume that intuition is just a foggy, emotional and confused form of thinking. Indeed, this view of intuition dominates in the world today. It is because this view is so widely held that it has been necessary to address the dominance of logic throughout the book.

And yet even those most convinced by logic cannot deny that intuitive thinking plays an important part in our major decisions and judgements. We use intuition for such decisions because life itself is rarely black and white. We use it to understand other people, for the very reason that people are not logical, and we use intuition to understand ourselves, not least because there is much about our own inner life which is inherently illogical, irrational, emotional and unconscious.

If there is little understanding of what intuition is and what it does, it is because it is ignored in favour of logic. This means that if we want to understand intuition, we have to pay specific attention to it. We have to study it and understand it, to think about it and to practice it where possible. For those who have succeeded in logic, this will seem pointless and time wasting. For those who have already begun to see the limitations of logic, this will be a first step to correcting a very real imbalance.

We believe we are free to do as we please. If we were not free, we would be no more than robots or machines. To be free, we have to be able to decide what we will or will not do. To decide freely, we have to be able to control our thinking. If we cannot do this, then what we regard as making a decision may be no more than an automatic reaction to an outer event. This would make our notion of freedom an illusion. There is a simple test to see whether you are in control of your thoughts or not. All you have to do is to prevent your mind from answering the following question. Once again, the test is to try to stop your mind from answering the question; if you cannot stop your mind from answering the question, then you cannot control your thoughts. So here is the question: what day comes after Monday?

What we call 'thinking' is often no more than following the thoughts that pass through our mind, rather like we might watch the passing scenery through the window of a train. To think, to actually think, means to be able to govern our thoughts, and to govern our thoughts we have to be able to monitor and control them. This is the function of intuition, or the watching mind. If we find ourselves reading a book and thinking about something else, or daydreaming on a train, or nodding in agreement while not really listening to what a person is saying, it is because the intuitive mind is passive. Sometimes we can even go through whole periods of time like this.

Having outlined the nature of intuition and having gone into some detail about its nature and applications, it is now possible to say something about the methods that arise through the direct application of intuition. Many have been hinted at throughout the book, but it will now be possible to state them more directly.

The first step towards developing the intuitive mind is to take an active interest in it. Reading a book such as this is a start, but if it is to become more than just a passing interest it must become a daily practice. Just as a person born with a natural musical ability cannot hope to turn this into a skill without practice, so a person born with a natural intuitive ability will find it at best unreliable without sufficient practice and attention.

The criticism of logic that runs throughout this book is not without reason. Because logic is the dominant form of thinking, in order to think intuitively we have to be able to hold off the persistence of the logical mind if we are to allow the intuitive mind to come to the fore. As with the above example of the asked question, the logical mind will supply the answer unless the intuitive mind is active enough to prevent it from doing so. The development of intuition does not mean that we reject logic, but merely that we begin to see it as only one form of thinking. Becoming aware of the dominance of logic, its nature and its methods is essential for the development of intuition.

When we think of autumn, for example, we think of the images of autumn which are most obvious and apparent to us. If we want to broaden our experience of autumn, we have to prevent our mind from thinking in terms of definitions and labels. To do this we have to try and still the logical mind. We may have had the experience of looking at a work of art and becoming aware of how the chattering mind prevents us from being able to take it in fully. If we can prevent the logical mind from interpreting experience, we may find that new thoughts arise which can provide useful insights into the hidden or less obvious elements of the experience. We can gain much from silent observation.

The most common form of intuition is what is called 'gut-feeling'. Gut-feeling is the dim realisation that something exists that we cannot see or state directly. Gut-feeling will draw our attention to this hidden element without telling us exactly what it is. This hidden element may be external, such as when we have the gut-feeling that someone is trying to deceive us, or it may be internal, such as when we are about to make a decision without examining our motives for making it. Gut-feeling draws our attention to what we are not seeing directly, or seeing only partially. This is why there was a chapter on illusion; what we see is often only part of a much greater whole. Gut-feeling will prompt us to consider the greater whole. If we pay attention to gut-feeling, we can begin the process of actively searching for what the hidden element might be.

Because intuitive thinking is inclusive, it allows us to consider different points of view, contradictory ideas and complex situations. Intuitively we know that we can partly agree with someone without having to fully accept or reject what they say. Intuitive thinking allows us to listen to one explanation, and then listen to a contrary explanation, and to accept that both will be partially true and both partially limited. The ability to listen to different points of view, to consider more than one perspective, and to look for more than one explanation is intuitive. This can become a deliberate practice, and indeed it must be practiced deliberately in order to become effective.

We do not simply observe the world around us, like a camera or a recording device, but we do so because it engages our interest, and that means it engages us emotionally. That is why an event, a person or a phenomenon can fascinate, irritate or puzzle us. This emotional element is overlooked by logic, and yet it clearly has an impact on what we attend to and what we ignore. In order to see this emotional element in our thinking, we have to observe our inner life intuitively. If we feel conflicting emotions, or if we feel uncertain about a decision, it is better to acknowledge this rather than attempt to eradicate it by applying limited logic. This does not mean we give in to our emotions, but simply that we acknowledge they exist.

To think intuitively therefore means that we have to be able to pick up on our moods, the moods of others, and the wider mood of the context we find ourselves in. This can become a deliberate practice. Becoming aware of our moods and emotions does not mean we become subjective and irrational, but actually the opposite; we cannot observe anything properly, whether it is people, life or nature, and be blind to what is going on in our inner life.

The most important distinction between logic and intuition is that logic deals with what we know and intuition deals with what we do not know. When we are confronted by an enigma, we can apply logic and dismiss it, or we can apply intuitive thinking and explore it for what it might tell us. An enigma is an indication that we do not see the world in its entirety, and that there is still much which is presently hidden from us. We can regard people, events, the laws of nature or even our own inner life as enigmas. By adopting this approach, our intuition will allow us to see beyond the simple labels of logic and the existing dogmas of the day. The study of enigmas is useful training for the intuitive mind.

Perhaps the most complete expression of intuitive thinking is insight. Whereas gut-feeling is vague and imprecise, insight is sharp and clear. Intuitive thinking begins with gut-feeling, or with the vague impression that there is something we are not seeing fully. If this feeling is pursued, and pursued intuitively, it can lead to insight. This can range from lesser insights, such an insight about a person's hidden motives, to insights about our own unconscious motives, and even to greater insights about the nature of the world. The effect of an insight can be overwhelming, and it can be accompanied by a feeling of elation or catharsis, particularly if it embraces into a single whole the many different elements that previously we thought were unconnected and even contradictory.

None of this can happen overnight. We have been so trained to think logically that we may find ourselves resorting to logic long after we have understood and seen its limitations. Our understanding of intuition has to be more than theoretical, but based on familiarity, direct experience and deliberate practice. Theoretical explanations are the product of logic, and they only serve to lead us further away from intuition rather than helping us to develop it. That is why this book makes no attempt to appeal to academics or philosophers.

The aim of this book has been to outline the basics of intuitive thinking. This has been done in light of the dominance of logic in society, in education and in culture. In a different context it would have been possible to say more about intuition, and much more directly. Perhaps in time it may be possible to do this.

Having an interest in intuition does not make us better people, nor does it mean we will always make the right decisions or judgements, nor does it mean we will always be free of deception or illusion. It just means that we will be able to see more, and see it more clearly, and then be able to deal with it on that basis. The world is a fascinating book if we know how to read it.

We ignore our intuitive mind at our own cost. If we allow our thinking to be governed by logic, we will be more certain of our opinions and judgements, but at the cost of limited perception. The hallmark of a foolish person is that they see too little and know too little and never suspect it. Our better decisions and judgements are intuitive because they are based on seeing more rather than seeing less. That is why intuitive thinking matters; we have to live with the consequences of our decisions and judgements, and any decision based on limited thinking is unlikely to be a good one.

Copyright

Printed in Poland
by Amazon Fulfillment
Poland Sp. z o.o., Wrocław

61878541R00103